The Parrot Who Owns Me

The

Story of a

Relationship

Joanna Burger

RANDOM HOUSE TRADE PAPERBACKS and colophon are trademarks of
Random House, Inc. This work was originally published in hardcover
in slightly different form by Villard Books in 2001.

Library of Congress Cataloging-in-Publication data is available.

ISBN 0-375-76025-3

Random House website address: www.atrandom.com

Printed in the United States of America on acid-free paper

24689753

First Trade Paperback Edition

Book design by Barbara M. Bachman

For all the parrots in the wild:

May we allow, encourage, and

help them and their habitats

survive in a world we have

the power to destroy.

And to the generations of students

who have taught me the importance

of drawing parallels between

animal behavior

and human behavior.

CONTENTS

The

Parrot

Who

Owns

Me

In Springtime His Thoughts Turn to Love

MY PARROT, TIKO, DIDN'T COURT ME UNTIL FIVE YEARS into our relationship. I knew how attached he was to me, but it came as a complete surprise when one morning in early April his behavior toward me suddenly changed. I found his diminutive brightly feathered self on my bed, insistently poking his head under my hand to solicit preening. In the past, he'd had the good manners to perch on the banister outside the bedroom, patiently watching me sleep and waiting until I stirred before coming in for his ritual morning preening, which had typically lasted five to ten minutes.

That morning Tiko gently picked at my cuticle and fingernails with his tongue and beak for two hours while I drifted in and out of sleep, dreaming of jungles, jaguars, and brilliantly colored parrots flitting through the forest canopy. After breakfast, bleary from interrupted sleep, I started work. I'm a biologist, a professor at Rutgers

University, and my specialty is ornithology. Tiko is a Red-lored Amazon, a distinguished member of a widespread Central American species. He has taught me a tremendous amount about bird behavior, but that's not why I have a perch for him in my home office. I enjoy his company, and usually he's a most considerate companion, valiantly standing guard over me, a silent sentinel, occasionally emitting a warning cry to protect me from the hawks he sees circling outside our picture window in Somerset, New Jersey.

But that spring morning, Tiko flew from his perch in my office, landed on my computer keyboard, and stomped over the keys, forcefully nudging my fingers away from their task. Even pinyon nuts, his favorite treat, did not deflect his desire; within moments he was back at my side. He began to make low mewing and moaning sounds that I hadn't heard before, while gazing pleadingly into my eyes. When I looked away, his mews and moans intensified until I reestablished eye contact. He gently nipped me with his beak—a kind of parrot kiss called "billing"—which I recognized from observing wild birds. He put his head flat against the desk, exposing his neck and hiding his beak.

I massaged the creamy skin on his nape, through feathers that are a pale sagebrush color tinged with electric blue. His skin is softer than a newborn baby's and very warm to the touch. Exposing his nape is a gesture of complete vulnerability: hawks and other predators target it for the kill.

After a few days of this, my husband, Mike, who has a Ph.D. in biology as well as being an M.D., and I suspected that Tiko was exhibiting classic male courting behavior. Our suspicions were confirmed when he began to scour the house for nest sites. He inspected the dark tight spots beneath our armchairs, couch, and television, behind books in the bookshelves, between the file cabinet and the daybed where I work in my office. Silent and intent, he spent only a minute or two in each place before flying back to stomp over my keyboard and nuzzle my hand.

I knew my parrot and I were close, but just how close, I was about to discover. Tiko finally chose the narrow slot under the credenza for what turned out to be "our" nest. The credenza is made of reddish cherry wood, about five feet long and waist high, with three low doors that open to cupboards, and drawers for silverware and napkins. Its bottom is a scant two inches off the floor. Tiko scrunched almost flat on his stomach to slither underneath it, and huddled there for long periods. God knows what he was thinking. When I ventured near, he gave a guttural cry.

"Hi, sweetie! What are you doing?" My voice held the lilting tone I would use with a five-year-old child. Even though Tiko was entering middle age—thirty-five years old in 1990, when this occurred—he responded well to being talked to and treated like a child. And, as we'll see, his behavior and intelligence were remarkably like a precocious three-year-old's.

That was, of course, before he became the *hombre* of the house, the passionate lover, the Don Juan of Somerset. His cries grew louder and he started growling, which sounded like the distant lowing of cattle. He peeked out from under the credenza, fixed me with his eyes, moaned enticingly, and ducked back into the darkness. He dashed to my toes, which he maniacally preened, hopped around my feet, then scooted back to the nest.

I knew from observing parrots both in the wild and in the lab that he was exhibiting what we ornithologists call "male nest-showing" behavior. I once watched this ritual in La Selva, a Costa Rican rain forest. Mike and I were on our way to the dry tropical forests of Palo Verde to study vigilance behavior in basking Black Iguanas, but we couldn't resist a quick detour to check up on Tiko's wild brethren.

We stayed at a research station run by the Organization for Tropical Studies (a consortium of universities), on whose board I served. Our spartan wood cabin was nestled into the edge of the jungle. We lit mosquito coils and settled into our bunk-bed cots, which were attached to the walls and so couldn't be pushed together. We lay under thin sheets, talking, as we always do, about the day, before drifting off to sleep.

We rose early to avoid the heat and made our way slowly along a winding path. The lowland tropical rain forest was thick with layers of vegetation. A rich leaf litter covered the jungle floor, the trees rising out of it tall and dense. We kept our eyes peeled for the deadly Fer-de-lance, one of the most feared and dangerous snakes in Central America and tropical Mexico. Unlike other vipers, which retreat when approached, the Fer-de-lance will strike if disturbed. Its dark mottled pattern blends perfectly with the jungle floor. We took our time, stopping now and then to focus our binoculars on the birds that fluttered through the canopy.

We walked for a couple of hours, often stopping to watch manakins, warblers (some of the same species that migrate north), brightly colored tanagers. When we were about three miles in, the dense forest opened and we found ourselves on the edge of a clearing where a storm had felled the larger trees. After the jungle gloom the clearing was light and airy; the early slanting sun created a patchwork brightness over the jumble of snags and green shoots. We smelled decaying undergrowth, wet leaves, and the sweet odor of rotting figs strewn near us on the ground. The figs were brownish-black, smaller and less fleshy than our domesticated ones, a favorite parrot food. Some of my colleagues have tried them; they're less sweet than our cultivated varieties. But if you were starving, they'd do quite nicely. The perfume of rainy-season flowers was heavy in the air and hummingbirds hovered at the lovely Heliconia, or Bird of Paradise, with its twisting yellow blooms, and the bromeliads that wound through the canopy, their leaves festooning the treetops.

The drone of cicadas was suddenly broken by the screeches and calls of two dozen parrots flying overhead. Each mated pair in the flock flew only a few inches apart, moving at great speed in perfect tandem. The birds were compact green missiles: their blunt green tails extending behind them gave them the appearance of powerful arrowheads, perfectly suited for flight, unlike their stubby, toppling gait on the ground. Their journey was filled with a loud chatter that took me back to Tiko. A pang of longing for him mingled with delight for his wild brethren, flying free in search of fruit and fresh blossoms.

Mike and I slipped into the shadows at the edge of the clearing and sat on a fallen log, hidden by the broad leaves of a banana tree. A pair of parrots peeled off from the flock, swooped down, and landed on a snag at the edge of the clearing. We wondered fleetingly if a hole in the dead tree was an old nest site of theirs. Wild parrots are shy; if they had known we were there they would have melted into the wall of green, but they were unaware of our presence. Parrots have sharp sight and keen hearing but a poor sense of smell, so all we had to do was keep quiet and still to remain undetected. Mike and I grasped hands in excitement.

It was very still in the clearing. The female stood coyly silent and immobile. She watched the male sidestep with a slight bobbing motion of his head; his lead leg extended like a dancer's along the branch on which they were perched. With a backward glance at her, he hopped down to a small opening in the trunk of the tree. He turned his head from side to side, then pecked tentatively at the hole's edge, dislodging a small piece of bark, which he flung over his shoulder, giving him the opportunity to glance back at his mate, who was watching his every move. He walked slowly back toward her, his head held low, neck feathers slightly erect, just the way Tiko would approach me during our courtship seasons. By the time he reached her, his bill was tucked neatly under his chin and his eyes were half closed.

The pair was silent. Mike and I whispered together, marveling at how the male's behavior mirrored Tiko's when he approached me for preening. The pair must have been well established or the male would not have placed himself in such a vulnerable position. How similar to human beings! I glanced at Mike, remembering the heady but often tense first years of our marriage, as we built the bond of trust that these wild birds displayed.

With a sideways glance the female turned toward the male and began to tentatively preen his neck feathers. He lowered his cream-colored eyelids until we glimpsed only a sliver of his yellow irises through our field glasses. Soon, the female swiveled her head, lifted a wing slightly, and began to run her bill through her own back feathers, indicating to him that it was his turn to preen her.

He sidled up and delicately extended his bill, making his intentions clear without intruding. I was moved by his discretion, his lack of presumption. Although she had given him a clear cue that she wanted to be touched, his attitude indicated—dare I say it?—consideration for her wishes; something akin to respect.

The female parrot drooped her head until her bill brushed the branch. He slowly began to preen her feathers, taking each one delicately in his hooked bill, sweeping it clear of dust and dirt. He dabbed his bill into a special gland at the base of his tail, picking up a small amount of oil, with which he coated her feathers. The oil is very fine, light, and odorless, so subtle it is hardly noticeable. It helps feathers stay supple and strong, and keeps the barbs interlocked so they repel rain. Nearly all birds have this oil, since they rely on feathers not just for flight but for insulation.

The male preened her for much longer than she had preened him (a precedent clearly established in the animal kingdom—it's the male's job to be more solicitous than the female). With eyes completely closed, she was content to rest her head on the branch. They remained this way, in a serene tableau, the male rhythmically running his bill through her plumage, she standing perfectly still in what looked to us like a swoon or trance. There was nothing bestial about the elaborate courtship between these two wild birds. There was a tenuous delicacy about it, subtle gradations of feeling.

Suddenly, the male bird broke off. The female's eyes opened and turned skyward. Mike and I glanced at each other, perplexed. Then we heard the distinctive cries of approaching parrots. They were suddenly upon us and as quickly gone.

He turned to face her, but the mood was broken.

Mike and I were disappointed that we were not about to see the pair engage in the more advanced stages of courtship. But we both knew as scientists that we had been incredibly lucky to see as much as we had. Observing parrots in the wild is often impossible: they're always on the move and live high in the jungle canopy, a wing-beat away from the sky.

The female vigorously preened her own feathers. The male scanned the edge of the clearing, on the lookout for jungle cats. I felt in their attitudes a restlessness, an imminent sense of departure. Perhaps they were reminded that it was still early morning, the best and quietest time to feed in the treetops, when it was not as hot as later in the day and there weren't likely to be hawk eagles riding the updrafts of warming air, sending parrots rocketing in panic to distant parts of the forest. Without a backward glance at the potential nest site, they leaped from the branch, pumped their wings, and soared up over the canopy and out of sight.

As I walked back to the cabin, my elation at seeing the wild parrots go through their age-old courtship dance turned to wistfulness. This was a part of his wild nature Tiko would never have the chance to experience. Were Mike and I somehow stunting Tiko, keeping him from his full potential? We talked this through in our cabin that night by lantern light, the wild sounds of the jungle around us. In our hearts we knew Tiko would love the tropical forest, but we also knew that releasing him would mean a certain death sentence. He would never survive, unable to find food, unsure how to avoid predators. Even given the slim chance he could learn to manage this entirely new environment, he might not be able to shift allegiance from me to another mate, and without a mate he would find life intolerable. Poor parrot, we ruefully laughed: stuck with a middle-aged ornithologist!

When a parrot or macaw gives its heart, that's it. Evidence abounds of their devotion. What was believed to be the last Spix's Macaw in the wild, a male, was paired to a female parrot of another species, and the pair could produce no young. Scientists introduced a captive female Spix's into the male's territory: remnant woodland near the São Francisco River in the northeastern province of Bahia in Brazil. They hoped he would recognize her as one of his own, abandon his unsuitable mate, breed with the new female, and produce the beginnings of a new wild stock of Spix's. Nothing doing! Love and loyalty won out over the arranged marriage. The captive female disappeared, much to everyone's chagrin.

Parrots are as choosy as people: personality seems to determine their choice of mates. It's not uncommon for parrots to mate with members of the same sex, and these homosexual couples will go through the same courtship dance and mating rituals as heterosexual pairs.

Parrots are not the only birds to couple up with members of the same sex. Female gulls in colonies where the sex ratio is so unbalanced that they cannot find a mate bond with other females. One or both of the paired females copulate surreptitiously with a male when its mate isn't looking, and then the paired females lay eggs in their own nest and take turns incubating the eggs and raising the chicks.

Mike and I left La Selva the next morning to observe the Black Iguanas. One of the things the fieldwork showed was that the iguanas' alarm response was triggered by our eyes. When I donned a mask with large black rings painted around the eyes, the iguanas startled at much greater distance than without the mask. I kept thinking of Tiko's expressive eyes: flashing when angry, or gazing intently into mine when he was feeling intimate.

I felt the weight of my responsibility for him; he relies on me for food, shelter, and companionship. The wild parrots of La Selva are free within the confines of preserves; but they too have humans guarding them, keeping the jungle free from poachers and logging. Tiko, lord of the roost in his Somerset home, is a microcosm of the predicament of wildlife all over the world: their future is in our hands.

THE WILD PARROT COUPLE in La Selva had broken off their amorous interactions before the male could induce the female to enter the hole in the snag he had found for them. In the parrot world, males often find and prepare the nest, while the females choose whether to accept it.

Our credenza in Somerset was hardly a hole in a forest tree, but this was the site on which Tiko settled, perhaps because it was near the kitchen; while I fixed meals I would coo at him. The credenza also had the advantage of being in full view of the kitchen's central island, where I chopped vegetables and cooked our meals. Perhaps my frequent eye contact with Tiko while he displayed at this site cemented his choice. I was delighted that he chose such a visible and convenient spot. I was fascinated by his courting behavior: as a scientist, it put me in the extraordinary position of not just an observer but a participant in Tiko's behavior.

One evening while I was preparing dinner, Tiko grabbed a section of newspaper off the dining room table and dragged it to the credenza. What's he up to? I wondered. He held the newspaper in one foot, shredded it with his beak, and carried some of this confetti into the nest. He emerged, growled at me, dashed into the kitchen, frenetically preened my toes, raced back under the credenza, and seductively cooed. Who could resist him? I was filled with gratitude that he'd seized on newspaper with which to make our "bed," rather than on the papers strewn over every surface of my office.

I lay down next to our nest. The distinct musty perfume of parrot seeped from the space and mixed with the smell of the dusty carpet. Tiko quickened the tempo of his calls. His tone was charged, hopeful, almost passionate. I was touched by his desire for my attention.

"Hi, sweetheart!" I said. "Is it a nice nest?"

The tenderness in my tone sent him running wildly back and forth, stopping here and there to delicately bill the rug. I wondered how to respond to this behavior, so full of excitement and longing, and I tentatively slipped my hand into the slot. He rushed to it, avidly preening my fingers and touching me softly with his tongue. I removed my hand and he rushed out, staring at me and crooning until I placed my fingers back into the nest.

The feel of his hard tongue against my fingertips was so gentle and soft. His bill was open; it, too, fondled my fingers. His touch was caressing, almost sensual. I could tell from his soft cooing that he was clearly in ecstasy. To my surprise I found that I was slightly squeamish.

Raised on a farm, I had learned the facts of life early. As a biologist I had spent many hours observing the sexual habits of birds, mammals, and reptiles. Prior to this point, I had found his courtship of me charming and fascinating, although his constant need for attention was a bit trying at times. But as he ran his tongue over my fingers under the credenza, I realized for the first time how serious he was, and I found that vaguely unnerving. I was exciting to him, even thrilling. My feelings for him were warm and fuzzy, difficult to describe. I retreated into my role of scientist, observing his behavior and stashing it for later analysis. But I was uneasy, as though I had transgressed an ancient taboo. His calls were low in his throat, a kind of purring, his tongue ardent and infinitely gentle on my knuckles.

I hadn't heard Mike enter the room, but I did hear him say, "What are you doing, Joanna?" I quickly retracted my hand as Tiko rushed at Mike's feet, head held low, wings slightly extended. Mike had the bad luck to be barefoot; he danced away as Tiko's beak went like a jackhammer for his toes.

"It's okay, sweetie," I reassured Mike. "Tiko was just courting me."

At the warm placating tone of my voice and, perhaps, my use of the endearment I typically reserve for him, Tiko launched himself from the floor and flew silently as a stealth bomber into Mike's face, nipping at his ears and neck. As Mike retreated upstairs, Tiko dashed back under the credenza, mewing and growling, hoping, no doubt, that I would reinsert my hand into "our" nest.

During this first mating season (and every mating season thereafter), Tiko was ferociously jealous of Mike, especially when Mike was affectionate with me. A mere hug from Mike brought Tiko to Mike's shoulder with threatening calls. Tiko tugged his hair and nibbled his ear, and this quickly escalated to a painful blood-drawing bite if Mike persisted.

More ardent advances turned Tiko frantic. When Mike gently kissed my supine body, Tiko landed on his naked back, wildly pecking him. Tiko stopped briefly to peer into my eyes and preen my hair. Then he flew madly around the room, returned to Mike's back, and ran up and down his body, calling loudly and pecking until we could soothe him by moving apart.

We would shut Tiko out of the bedroom for our more heated moments. He would fly to the room farthest from ours, and when I went to put him in his cage for the night I would find him staring out the window. This became the place he went only when Mike and I were together in our bedroom with the door closed. If I was alone, he waited patiently outside the door for me to emerge.

Many of my parrot-owning friends report similar behavior when they are affectionate or, even worse, when they make love. They go to great lengths to keep their parrots from suspecting that these "indiscretions" occur. Like me, they put their parrot to bed in a room far from their bedroom, amid cooing and reassurances that the parrot is their sweetheart. Under cover of darkness their parrots sleep, blissfully assuming their "mates" do, too. It's unclear whether parrots are being jealous or just protective. But the result is the same. The parrot must be banished from the room.

For the most part, I find Tiko's mating-season antics amusing, although they can sometimes be tough on Mike. Occasionally, a small sigh of exasperation escapes his lips when, for example, Tiko shrieks in horror and attacks should Mike have the audacity to appear in the doorway of our office after showering, wrapped only in a towel.

But fortunately, Mike doesn't take Tiko's behavior to heart. His scientific curiosity and compassion for Tiko far outweigh the inconvenience caused by Tiko's possessiveness. And Tiko is very close to Mike. His nips are, at first, cursory; only if Mike ignores them do they become painful, and even then they don't seem calibrated to do any lasting harm. Mike still has two ears. Tiko will often try to make up for his bad behavior by alighting on Mike's shoulder and initiating a whistling duet, something he does only with Mike. He whistles a phrase and Mike repeats it. When they have a piece they know, Mike will whistle a bar or two, stop, and Tiko will seamlessly pick up the piece. Tiko seems particularly fond of Baroque harpsichord music (Scarlatti is a favorite), and his repertoire is vast. His ability to mimic Mike's whistle is eerie: when I close my eyes I can barely tell their whistles apart.

During the rest of that spring, Tiko constantly tried to tempt me for yet another interlude under the credenza. Out of guilt, curiosity, and affection for him, I sometimes allowed myself to be seduced. He began to eye me reproachfully for not somehow squeezing my entire body into our nest. By the beginning of July, his breeding season was over, his ardor had waned, and we all returned to our routine.

THE NEXT MATING SEASON, I didn't know what to expect. As April rolled around, Tiko once again became fiercely attentive. He demanded long bouts of preening in bed each morning, attacked Mike at the slightest provocation, and rushed under the credenza whenever I was in the kitchen.

One spring evening he was perched on the refrigerator while I was making spaghetti sauce. With a flurry of wings he dropped to the counter and gingerly touched a piece of the onion with his tongue, trying to decide if it was safe to eat.

"Go ahead, sweetie. Try it!"

Reassured, he took a few bites, then switched to the green peppers I was chopping. Aromatic steam rose off the pan, absorbing my attention until I suddenly realized he was gone. Soft croons came from inside the black vinyl recliner in our living room, emanating from a hole five inches wide in the chair's back. Vinyl bits littered the floor. How had he known the chair was hollow? And why had he shifted nest sites? Had I shown insufficient interest in the credenza?

"Tiko, sweetheart, what are you doing in there?" His green head popped from the hole. Eyeing me, he ripped off a chunk of upholstery and flung it to the floor. What is one supposed to say at such a moment? How virile! I suppose he wanted to impress me with his industry. He savaged the chair a bit more to emphasize his point and climbed back into the hole with a rising croon that said, "Follow me!"

Reaching inside the chair I felt only space. Then, tentatively, my fingers fell upon its wooden frame, and traced the narrow slats that hold its arms. Delving into this dark webby place raised the hair on the back of my neck. Inside the chair the air was dead and warm. It was with relief that I touched the floor through the springs; but still no Tiko. Was he hurt? Enmeshed in the recliner's bowels?

Peering inside the hole I saw nothing. "Tiko, where are you? Where have you gone?" I began to worry.

He called from deep within and I followed his voice, finally touching him in the far corner of the seat, between springs and padding. I felt him turn and slowly begin to preen my fingers.

He was thrilled with our new nest and displayed there frequently. He worked diligently to enlarge its entrance, and it was useless to try to dissuade him. My one hope was that he would maintain interest in this particular site and not begin construction anew.

Whenever I was in the kitchen, he ran straight for the chair. He shredded it, heaving hunks of upholstery triumphantly to the floor. He sang in dizzy notes that rose and fell, resolving themselves into a long trilling call. Then, one evening, he started to do a very strange thing. Instead of running to the hole, he stiffly advanced, his head thrust forward, his neck feathers fluffed. He jerked his beak and throat, alternating these choking motions by pecking softly at the floor. The choking became more pronounced; he rapidly bobbed his head back and forth, mandibulating his bill as if to bring something up; a strangled clucking sound escaped from his throat. I panicked. What had he swallowed? How do you give a parrot the Heimlich?

I was alarmed, afraid Tiko was choking to death, and ran to find Mike, who was outside gardening. We rushed back to the living room to find him quietly preening his tail feathers. He took one look at me, started choking again, and ran like a drunken man to the nest hole. This was obviously part of his courtship display, and he was really quite fine.

Mike knew better than to stick around and went back outside. I joined Tiko behind the chair. He gently billed my finger, choked in earnest, raised the feathers around his neck to form a ruff, and bobbed his head rapidly to the left and right, calling softly with each choking movement. He began regurgitating partially digested pinyon nuts into my hand, a real sign of devotion, since he loves these more than any other food. Finally, he secreted a milky substance on my fingers as he billed them softly. This sticky mess didn't exactly light my fire, and I withdrew my hand.

But, at the same time, I was quite amazed: Tiko was demonstrating his powerful bond with me. Many species of birds practice this behavior, which is called courtship feeding.

Courtship feeding is common in birds where both parents contribute to the care of their young. The male feeds the female prior to egg-laying and sometimes during incubation. She must eat enough to nourish herself, store nourishment in her eggs, and produce her clutch quickly. Unless the eggs are laid in quick succession, the young will be different sizes; the larger chicks will grab all the food, starving the smaller chicks and reducing the pair's reproductive success.

The male feeds the female so she can put all her energy into producing her clutch early in the breeding season. An early start gives the brood time to gain weight and learn to forage on their own before facing the pressures of the dry season, or of a hard winter and migration in the case of temperate-nesting species. Courtship feeding also allows the female to judge the male's ability to provide food for the young during the brood phase.

Unlike most birds, male parrots courtship-feed throughout the year; it is connected not only to sex and reproduction, but also to pair-bond maintenance. Indeed, parrots share this behavior pattern with humans—we are attentive to our mates regardless of the season. Or, at least, we should be. It was more likely that Tiko was courtship-feeding me to solidify our pair bond rather than to fatten me up before I laid eggs.

No matter how many times Tiko regurgitated on my hand or harried Mike, I was a complete dud as a mate. Our nest had no eggs. Tiko never lost interest, however, and made a madcap dash for the recliner in the living room whenever I was near it, enticing me with coos and pleading calls to stick my arm into our nest where he had regurgitated in it. This may sound at least faintly repulsive to humans, but we should keep in mind how similar our response is to that of a six-year-old's hearing, for the first time, about French-kissing. In the parrot world, regurgitation is a demonstration of love and intimacy reserved only for a mate. Although in our Somerset living room it seemed like the apex of foreplay, a prelude to going all the way, in the wild the behavior is much more complex and not restricted only to the last stages of activity before coitus.

Lacking a truly responsive mate, Tiko never copulated. This seemed not to bother him; he remained happy and good-natured. He flew willingly to my shoulder whenever I appeared, and contentedly preened my hair to indicate that all was well.

All species of parrots copulate in the same way, and I was alert to any sign that Tiko was making a run for home plate. Observing copulation in wild parrots is difficult because they are so shy and reclusive. For many, many years I had searched for it, but at that time the closest I'd come was watching Peach-faced Lovebirds, a species of parrot, copulate in the laboratory. I filled their cages with plants and small trees, which cost me a fortune but were worth it. With a wall of green between us they forgot about me and mated.

The female lovebird initiated sex by sidling up to her mate, who placed a foot on her back while his other foot clutched their perch. She lowered her body until it was prone, raised her tail, and withdrew her head and neck slightly into her body feathers. She quivered her wings and uttered a low cackling sound. He moved his foot lower on her back and swung his tail under hers so their two cloacas (genital areas) touched. As they pressed together he pumped his tail, transferring sperm to her.

Tiko has never had this experience, which for most of us is such a central part of being alive. As I've mentioned, I've on occasion considered introducing him to a female bird, but parrots bonded to human beings typically disdain other parrots. Friends have acquired second parrots with horrific results; the two birds detest each other, screech nonstop, and need to be caged in separate rooms. Parrots are emotionally fragile. Breaking Tiko's bond with me and inducing him to bond with a female parrot would be risky and an enormous investment of time.

In captivity, some male birds will mount and "mate" with a variety of objects. We once had a pet Shiny Cowbird, which Mike had rescued as a baby from the pampas of Argentina. Mike snatched it from a roadside nest about to be mowed by a road crew. Minutes later the nest was destroyed, the resident female left to renest in a safer location. (Actually, the resident female was a Red-breasted Meadowlark; cowbirds always lay their eggs in the nests of other birds, a practice called "parasitism.") Shiny Cowbirds range from the West Indies to Argentina but have recently invaded North America and are now nesting in Florida. They are aggressive, pugnacious, and a potential pest species, though Mike's cowbird was a joy to have in the house.

Each spring, he became an avid mounter. Almost anything at a forty-five-degree angle was sufficient to initiate the act. I could even induce him to mount my bare foot by dangling it near and raising it provocatively. When he was ready to mount he would peck vigorously at my foot or wrist, until I raised it to the appropriate position, whereupon he would hop on, wiggle his tail, and deposit a bit of semen. One grows tired of such behavior over a period of time. Fortunately, Tiko has never gone this far, and I really don't know how I would respond if he attempted to mount my hand. I get carried away by my research, but this might be too strange even for the sake of science. On the other hand, I might feel obliged to submit.

Each April since that initial spring, Tiko's heart turns to "love" and he searches for an appropriate nest site. He is always faithful to the old ones, returning to display there now and again, but he also adds new ones, perhaps since the previous year's site proved fruitless. He has a special nest site under some piece of furniture in almost every room: a dresser, chair, bookshelf, desk, or credenza. In the wild, parrots use the same nest trees year after year as long as they are free from predators; Tiko has continued the tradition in his own "tropical forest" in Somerset. However, since I never really accept his nests, he explores new ones, ever hopeful that he will find one that satisfies me.

In recent years, Tiko has become even more amorous, extending the season of courtship well into the summer. I suppose I should feel flattered; his possessiveness knows no bounds. For fully half the year Mike has to tread softly and act the role of rather distant platonic friend when Tiko is around. It's an odd ménage à trois, even for suburban Somerset.

It wasn't always this way. In fact, the road to intimacy with Tiko was long and arduous. And strange as it may seem, I was to learn that his desire to mate with me did not signal the deepest reserves of the trust and love of which I now know he is capable. Tiko has taught me much about parrots, birds in general, and our relationship with the animal kingdom. And he has also taught me profound lessons in what it means to be human. But first I had to learn about the true nature of parrot-human relations.

I thought when Tiko came to live with me that it was I who owned him. I can't believe I was ever so deluded! I admit it—I was sorely in need of training. When I look back on those early days, it is with a sense of wonder that I could have ever been such a fool.

2

The Journey North

BEFORE TIKO CAME TO LIVE WITH ME, I HAD HEARD about him for years. His home was in Florida with two retired sisters, whose Yiddish locutions he'd adopted and whose every meal he shared. Our neighbor Josie (daughter of one sister, niece of the other) would return from a trip to Florida, often the worse for wear, and regale me with tales of Tiko's behavior. He spoke an unfathomable parrot Yiddish. Was that *"Oy gevalt!"* he squawked as the sisters *kvelled* over his charm and beauty? No one was sure.

"I think I know what the problem is," she told me once. "He never liked me after my mother made me take him to the vet, and this last visit things got completely out of hand." We commiserated over the low, vine-covered fence that separated our backyards.

It was the fateful summer of 1983 when Tiko and Josie had their falling out. Tiko was at his most difficult and irate. Josie had been making her bed, about to go into a sedate breakfast with her elderly relations. Tiko careened through the door of the her room and went straight for her head. She fell back, covered her face with the sheet, and flailed at him. Tiko bobbed and weaved like Joe Louis, flew off, circled the ceiling several times, picked his opening, then dove like the bird of prey into which he had transformed, swooping in under the hysterical flutterings of her flimsy shield and sinking the wire clipper of his beak—a compact layer of epidermal cells molded around a bony core—into the most tender part of her ear.

We can perhaps forgive her shriek of terror as blood spurted from the wound onto the white sheet.

"It sounds like something out of Hitchcock!" I said as she relayed the story.

"I was absolutely helpless," Josie said. "My mother scooped up Tiko and consigned him to his cage. He sat there on his perch, glaring triumphantly at me. I swear to you, those beady eyes of his were full of hate."

"How extraordinary. Perhaps if you tried talking gently to him? Butter him up. Throw in a Yiddish phrase or two." I injected hope into my voice, but I knew that once a parrot conceived a distaste for you, the game was usually over. Their memories are long, and their prejudices difficult to fathom or alter. And, I had to admit secretly, at least part of my sympathies were for this fearless, spirited bird. God alone knew why Tiko's dislike for Josie had escalated into open warfare, but on her subsequent trips to Florida, following the bed-making episode, Tiko was confined to his cage.

I listened raptly to Josie's stories. She knew birds were my passion; parrots, my weakness. My love for birds went back to childhood, the beginning of memory. I wandered as a little girl through the woods behind our family farm in Mohawk Valley, New York, thrilled by the Great Blue Herons that stood motionless on one leg while they scanned the water for carp or catfish. I could scarcely believe the still, stately creatures were living beings, able to stand with their heads so far extended without toppling over. Then suddenly the head would shoot forward, the neck uncoiling like a spring. The beak clasped a wriggling, flapping fish. The heron would flip the fish around in its beak until it was facing head first. The bird jerked its head back, swallowing the fish in one gulp, the slippery scales sliding down its gullet. And then it came back again to rest, stately in its stance, its profound stillness. Or, without warning, it would extend its wings upward, push off with its legs, and rise in flight with one or two powerful flaps of its great smoke-colored wings, its long legs hanging off its body, trailing through the sky like streamers on a kite.

The loud hammering of a Pileated Woodpecker was a sound I could never resist; it drew me deep into hardwood forests that rose up from the river valley. I searched out its source in the summer heat, in the quivering kaleidoscope of green leaves overhead. The standing snag was pocked and grooved, excavated by the jackhammer beak as the woodpecker searched for beetles and grubs, the oblong hole a sure indication of its work. There was formality to the bird's tuxedo colors that was broken by the flash of red on the crest of the tufted head. Sometimes I wondered how the woodpeckers managed to pound so hard without damaging their brains. (I now know that their skulls are specially adapted to take the pressure.)

My mother, Janette, showed me my first American Bittern, hidden among the cattails. It stood motionless, its bill pointing straight at the sky, its streaked brown breast permitting it to blend perfectly with its surroundings. Sometimes I'd watch bitterns stand like statues for an hour, even longer than the herons did, without a flicker of movement to give them away. That sense of motionlessness is something I have carried with me when I've watched animals in the field. It is part of my science, my methodology. They were so well camouflaged that unless I chanced on one in the act of fishing it would take me forever to find them.

I reveled in the bullheaded energy of the woodpecker, the stealth and stillness of the fishing birds. In grade school I played hooky to watch flocks of crows in the fields, marveling at their curiosity and inventiveness. One of my tasks each summer was to chase them on horseback from my father's vegetable fields. I would ride the Thoroughbred my uncle Louie had given us, from just before dawn until dusk, endlessly circling the fields, the horse and I briefly sending the flocks of glossy black birds scattering.

I delighted in the flocks of Ring-billed Gulls when they passed over the farm each fall on their migration south, and when they appeared again in the spring, on their northbound journey. To a young girl the noisy dense flocks streaming after the plow in search of worms posed a tantalizing mystery. Where did they come from? Where were they going?

By the time I reached junior high in the mid-1950s, I was in the habit of bringing home injured birds—baby Killdeer, robins, Redwinged Blackbirds, sparrows. I'd bring them to my room, place them gingerly in a shoe box lined with soft rags, and give them food and water until they were well enough to be released. Some died; to these I gave a solemn burial in the woods, marking each grave with a stone, on which I'd carefully print "Baby Robin," "Red-winged Blackbird," "Song Sparrow." After wishing the bird well and gently covering it with earth, I'd sit quietly at the graveside, mourning my departed friend. Though I was young, sex, birth, death, sadness, and sorrow were ingrained in my childhood, part of my farm legacy.

My family looked on bemused, but never interfered. A fair number of my birds recovered, and I'd take them to the spot where I'd picked them up, open the box, and watch them fly into the sky. My heart went with them, the momentary sadness at their disappearance turning into a profound joy at their freedom, their restoration to life.

In high school my father, Melvin, showed me a Killdeer nest, and I then discovered Killdeer and Spotted Sandpiper nests beneath my father's squash and tomato plants. I watched fascinated as the males and females alternated incubation duties. When the chicks hatched, I marked them with colored pens and followed them through the fields, plotting their location on a crude map. They could walk almost from birth, and wandered after their parents learning to feed. Their coloring was cryptic and they stayed in the cover of taller grasses, but with patience I managed to keep track of them. I was elated when they first took flight, although I missed them when they flew south for the winter.

My interest in birds deepened through college and graduate school. I wrote my doctoral dissertation at the University of Minnesota on the behavior of gulls, and I kept a number of birds as pets.

They proved to be wonderful companions. But by the early 1980s my energy was focused on my burgeoning career at Rutgers—I was developing new courses in animal behavior, ecology, and evolution, and a research program in the social behavior of birds and mammals. Between my career and my then-new husband, Mike, I was left with neither the time nor the energy to care for a feathered companion of my own.

Partly for this reason, I took enormous pleasure in Josie's tales of Tiko. I formed a picture of the bird as a curmudgeon with clout, a strong-willed, cantankerous character down in the subtropical wilds of central Florida who lorded over a household consisting of two doting Jewish ladies and himself.

BUT IN 1984, Tiko's world turned upside down. Josie's mother died, leaving him and Libby alone. For weeks after Freda's death Tiko sought her vainly, flying to all her favorite spots—the back of the wing chair she favored, the kitchen table where they'd shared countless meals, the top of her dresser mirror. He became less vocal, flew less. He stopped making the low cooing sound that signified contentment. He seemed as baffled as a child might be by the disappearance of a loved one, as depressed as a bereaved adult. He appeared to be in mourning, although Libby gave him more attention than he'd received from both sisters when Freda was alive, and he adored her.

Over time his mood improved somewhat, and he resumed picking bits of food from Libby's plate. Sometimes, when she scratched his head and neck, he would shut his eyes in ecstasy.

Then Libby, who was eighty-five, became ill.

Josie suggested that her aunt move to a nursing home up north. Libby saw the wisdom of having her niece close at hand, but she would not, to Josie's dismay, be parted from her companion of more than twenty-five years. Although a year had passed since Tiko had attacked Josie, it was the kind of experience that stayed in the mind. Nevertheless, the bird would be going north.

Aunt Libby refused to travel by plane—too much *mishegas* up there these days, she said—nor would she impose on Tiko the indignities of the baggage compartment. Josie made reservations on Amtrak; a sleeper was a necessity, both for Tiko and her aunt. It fell to Josie to buy and present Tiko with a new, smaller cage, suitable for train travel, and she made the effort to explain to him what was going on. Heeding my earlier advice, she says she wracked her brain trying to recall some fraction of what little Yiddish she had ever known.

"Tiko, *bubbeleh,* I know your new quarters are a little small, but believe me, when we get to Jersey, what I'll buy for you is a palace." He seemed attentive to her, even cordial, until it came time to put him in the cage. The usual method was to present him with a stick, onto which he would, more often than not, obligingly step. But he refused the stick when Josie offered it, and—a first for him—rejected Libby, too. Nor was he lured into the cage by an array of his favorite foods. Instead he took off, flying frantically around the house, and as Josie went after him (while Libby moaned and clutched her chest) his agitation grew. Pictures fell from the walls, vases overturned, papers flew. He took an occasional breather on the back of the sofa or the top of the fridge, but no amount of coaxing could persuade him to enter the small cage. It seemed as if he understood that eventually he would wind up in it, but what was the rush? Finally, perhaps recalling the crux of their relationship, he swooped low over the floor and veered upward into Josie's face. She ducked, just managing to evade another painful bite.

This sort of blast from the past she didn't need. Tiko's failure to inflict pain seemed to incite him further. He flew to a curtain rod and dive-bombed her again. She grabbed a large towel, wrestled him to the floor, and shoved the bundle into his cage. He struggled out of the towel's folds, smoothed his ruffled feathers, and glared at her menacingly.

They put the cage into a laundry bag, in which they'd keep him for the duration of the journey, and taxied to the train. In the dark, Tiko remained silent while they seated themselves in the compartment that they had procured so Tiko and Libby would have some privacy and comfort for the long ride. Josie tended to her aunt, who was having doubts, not entirely unfounded, about the quality of life in a nursing home. While she reasoned with the old woman, she was grateful that Tiko held his tongue.

They managed to fall asleep, shielded from the masses of college students on their way home from vacation and the kids excited by their visits to Disney World. A supercilious steward awoke them for lunch and sang the virtues of the seafood grazing tray, but they declined, and dined instead on the exquisite picnic of baked chicken, biscuits, and fruit they had packed from home.

"I just don't feel like eating. Maybe Tiko would like the chicken."

"I could check, I suppose. But I know he has enough food and water."

"We should have a look. He's too quiet by a long shot."

With little enthusiasm and very gingerly, Josie opened the laundry bag and peered at the cage within. There, on his perch, was a parrot; he appeared sentient, but paid her no heed. His eyes were closed, and he swayed gently with the moving train.

"He seems fine," she reported to her aunt. "He said 'No thanks' to the chicken."

The bird kept his own counsel as the long train rumbled north, palm trees and orange groves giving way to the signs of a bleak northeastern winter. Josie hoped—she hoped she hoped—that the bird would remain alive and well. He looked hardy, tough as nails. And he remained silent during the whole of the twenty-eight-hour trip, except when he mimicked his version of the moaning sound of the rumbling train. Occasionally she opened the cage to let light in so that he could eat, and when she thought no one would enter, she left it open for a while. They both were amused by his rendition of the roaring train and his side-to-side swaying.

When he was shrouded in darkness he was silent. The jungle is a dangerous place once the sun goes down; birds, wary of predators, fall silent. But his silence was also due to the strange sounds and smells, the movement of the train, the knowledge that he was being dragged against his will into the unknown. His acute sense of dislocation had catapulted him into a state of shock.

A parrot in a box is more troubled by its situation than a dog would be, because parrots are used to *constant* stimulation, need to eat more frequently than dogs, and, unlike dogs, are diurnal (active during the day). Josie's deep concern for her aunt prevented her from talking him through the trip—that, and her unfortunate history with the bird. The words would have been unimportant, but the right tone of voice might have done the trick. Wild parrots murmur softly to their mates and are strongly affected by even subtle shifts of tone in the human voice.

As it was, Tiko traveled a day and a night and well into the next day, enduring starts and stops, the sounds of footsteps nearby, and an endless stream of strange voices and smells, his world reduced to a tiny space. I see him huddled deep within himself, swaying gently to the moving train, mesmerizing himself into a state of suspended animation, wondering where he was going, and why.

NOT LONG AFTER she got back to Somerset and settled her aunt into the home (where pets, which might have done the residents a world of good, were not allowed), Josie invited Mike and me over for dinner. That was my first glimpse of Tiko. I had no way then of knowing the extent to which the meeting would change my life.

We let ourselves in through Josie's back door. Almost at once we heard a familiar sound—the eerie, thrilling call of an Amazon parrot, loud, harsh, and at a lower pitch than the calls of all other parrots but macaws. We quickened our pace up the stairs.

Josie was all smiles. "I can't wait for you to see him."

We passed through the kitchen into the small dining room, dominated by several large potted plants, their foliage trailing along the floor. Josie was doing what she could to mock up her notion of a jungle environment. A small cage stood on a stool. It was not hard to see what Tiko had been sounding off about—Josie's two large poodles stood like sentinels beneath the cage, staring up at him silently. It was unclear whether they were trying to decode his chatter or contemplating their next meal.

I stopped several feet away. I saw, clutching his perch, a medium-sized parrot. Most of his body was covered in feathers of different shades of green, which shifted subtly as he moved beneath the light. "He's beautiful," I whispered. He was pale green beneath, shading to olive on his wings. His cheeks were an iridescent green. His forehead was a vibrant red, and he had a small red patch on each wing. The top of his head and his hind neck feathers were tinged pale blue; his tail was yellow-green on the outer tips, with some red mixed in, but the innermost tail feather was solid green. The tips of his wings were black.

"Hello, Tiko," I said.

I resolved not to speak softly and sweetly to him, although it was an effort to be simply cordial, matter-of-fact. I was determined to avoid any tone or gesture he might consider friendly. I knew he felt abandoned by Josie's mother and aunt, and I did not wish to replicate the same feeling in him when we left. So I used a guarded tone, and avoided making eye contact. It pained me to be this remote; but given what I knew about this particular bird, it had to be done.

He sat hunched forlornly at the back of the cage with feathers fluffed and head withdrawn, but his eyes were intelligent and clear.

"He's beautiful!" I whispered again to Mike as Josie approached the cage with his dinner, a dish of parrot mix (seeds, nuts, Kix, and Cheerios). Tiko grunted and lunged forward. He flashed his eyes in anger, the pupils constricting while the bright irises expanded. One moment his eyes were black, rimmed with yellow; the next they flashed bright red. In the wild or in captivity, parrots flash their eyes when upset, or when feeling aggressive. It's a sign that they plan to attack, or at a minimum it says, "You'd best take me seriously." I was utterly astounded: here he was, wrenched from everything he knew and loved, yet still able to flash his eyes at the woman bringing him his food, merely because he wasn't crazy about her. I loved him at once for his spunk.

"I'm getting him a larger cage tomorrow," Josie said as we sat down to dinner. She sounded apologetic. "Back in Florida he had one four times the size." She truly wished Tiko well, yet they had never connected. Josie loved animals; she communicated easily with her poodles, petting them while she spoke to them. But, like most people, she didn't know that birds need a great deal of the same kind of attention. She felt silly sweet-talking a parrot, especially one that seemed to detest her.

During dinner, Tiko was subdued. Once the poodles wandered off he fell silent. He appeared lost in thought, some brooding parrot reverie on the mysterious language of canines, his adoption by a woman whom he clearly considered an adversary, and the bewildering, inexplicable disappearance of the two sisters he loved. Although he did nothing to draw attention to himself, I saw Mike, with a smile on his face, often look his way. He was clearly as taken with Tiko as I was.

"You know," Josie said, "they don't allow birds in the nursing home. If the doctors don't think Libby can recover and come live with me, I wonder——this is down the road, of course——would you consider taking Tiko?"

Mike and I smiled at each other.

"I hope Libby recovers," I said, wondering as I said it if I was being entirely honest. "But if things work out differently, we'd love to have him."

Underneath his lunging, ear-biting exterior I perceived a creature of indomitable spirit and high intelligence. I felt that with the proper environment and nurturing that I could give him, he would develop his full potential and become the kind of loyal and loving companion he had been to Josie's mother and aunt. Perhaps it was hubris on my part, but I felt he was crying out for the kind of informed attention that I, as an ornithologist, could give him. Sensing his pain and isolation, I was drawn back to my days as a girl when I took injured birds and nursed them back to health. Of course, when they were better I let them fly free. Tiko's injuries were of the heart, not the body, and he'd been born and raised in captivity, so letting him loose in the jungles of Costa Rica would have been his death sentence. Should Tiko come into our hands, both Mike and I were aware that he would most likely be a lifetime companion, for better or worse, in sickness and health. But we didn't hesitate that night, sitting around the dinner table at Josie's.

Why do we form the relationships we do? Why do we make the commitments we make, which define our lives? Mike and I hadn't even needed to confer about our willingness to have Tiko join our family. In large part, it was because we both love birds, and this joint passion for birds is at the root of our marriage. When Mike and I began our relationship, he'd had a Shiny Cowbird, the avid mounter I mentioned earlier, whose name was Moomoo. Mike's attachment to Moomoo was, to me, a rare and wonderful quality in a man, and helped our romance flourish. I first met Mike in 1973, at an American Ornithologists' Union meeting held on Cape Cod. We wandered the dunes together, looking for rare migrant birds. We became good friends. We shared a profound interest in ornithology, indeed in all of nature. For many years we visited each other's field sites, and one day, while in Mexico, we finally "discovered" each other. I was in no hurry to get married. It wasn't uncertainty about Mike that made me hesitate, but rather a certain skepticism about marriage as an institution. But he was unhappy not being married, and, since I was madly in love with him, I relented. We were married in 1981 on top of the two-thousand-year-old Dzibilchaltun pyramids, on Mexico's Yucatán Peninsula. I've never had reason to regret it.

Mike had studied meadowlarks and cowbirds in Argentina for his doctoral dissertation, and, after rescuing Moomoo from the road crew, flouting the quarantine, he smuggled the little black bundle back into the country, where we all lived happily in Somerset, New Jersey. Moomoo spent his days following us and our children, Debbie and David, around the house. When I went downstairs to ride my exercise bike, he would come along and sit on the windowsill, watching birds in the backyard. But one year, not realizing that Moomoo was in the room with me, Mike opened the back door. The bird flew outside, and as Mike cried, "Moomoo, no!" he took to the sky without so much as a backward glance. When a bird whose entire life has been spent in captivity gets loose, it will fly for a while, take a look around, and more often than not discover that it can't find its way home. We assume that this is what happened to Moomoo.

A devastated Mike haunted the yard for several days, calling over the rooftops to the sky, hoping the bird might wander close enough to hear his voice. There was not much I could do to comfort him; I brought food and drink, which he sometimes took, but mainly I let him be. Moomoo was twelve, old for a cowbird, and when he failed to reappear, Mike consoled himself with the thought that at least he'd had the chance, for his final months, to live free. We mourned him and then became immersed in our careers. The last thing we thought of was another bird. Until Tiko.

TRUE TO HER WORD, Josie bought Tiko a "palace," the Cadillac of birdcages, a shiny, gilded roost equipped with toys, bells, and a mirror. None of these doodads amused him. Even the mirror, which should have piqued his vanity, left him cold. The poodles still kept a vigil beneath his cage and peered up at him expectantly, occasionally sounding off. Parrots in captivity often bond with pet dogs, follow them around, even ride on their backs. Tiko called back to them with a wonderful poodle-bark rendition. But the dogs cocked their heads quizzically for a moment, and then went back to licking their chops.

And then the screeching started. Tiko, as morose Amazons in captivity are wont to do, began to scream. It was a wrenching, mournful cry of exasperation that went on and on, a protracted exorcism of the demon of loneliness lodged in his heart. I heard it when I left the house and worked in the garden. It even followed me for a considerable distance down the street. His voice had evolved to carry over acres of tropical forest, and now it easily pierced Josie's walls.

I understood the screeching to be an outgrowth of his loneliness. Josie was at work all day and no one was there to talk to him, even had Josie been so inclined. All the same, whenever I found myself in Tiko's presence, I continued my standoffish ways. Beyond my fears that he might think I had bonded with and then abandoned him was my conviction that the relationship couldn't be rushed. Your average parrot is not your average dog. Dogs have been bred to seek approval from just about anybody. Not parrots. You must go slow. Trust must be earned. Parrots want to make their own friends at their own speed; pushing them provokes fear or aggression. They have quick, wicked tempers. In the wild, I've watched them happily preen, strung out along a branch; suddenly, one bird will lunge at another for no apparent reason.

Even had I wished to befriend him, I would never, at that juncture, have put my hand into his cage. That would have constituted an unacceptable breach of boundaries, something like sticking your head into a stranger's car after he had rolled down his window to give you directions.

OVER THE NEXT MONTHS, whenever I visited Josie I looked in on Tiko. Each time his plumage was duller, and he seemed more lethargic and morose. He became increasingly despondent. And Josie looked haggard as well. "Is he sick?" she asked me. "I know he misses my mother, Libby, Florida. But he won't eat. He won't touch the fresh strawberries and raspberries you told me to feed him. You know I'm not crazy about him, but I'd like him to thrive, for my mother's sake. What should I do?"

"He'll be fine. He's just lonely." As an afterthought, I said, "I imagine he wouldn't mind flying around a bit."

"He'll go right for me!"

"Well, talk to him at least." I hadn't intended to reproach her, but she looked hurt.

"I don't know how to talk to a bird. Anyway, he doesn't like me."

"Maybe he'll learn to," I lied.

I promised her I'd come back soon to check on Tiko.

Late the following afternoon I got a call. "Joanna, come quickly, I'm afraid Tiko's hurting himself!"

I rushed over to her house and was ushered to the dining room. Behind its closed door the sound of a parrot's wing-beats were audible. There was a crash and glass shattering.

"How did it happen?" I asked, not sure I wanted to know.

It turned out that, following the sage advice of her neighbor the revered ornithologist, Josie had put the poodles out into the yard and let Tiko out of his cage. Surely, she reasoned, he had forgotten his old animosity. After all, she had been bringing him his food and water for months now, she'd procured for him the best cage money could buy, she talked to him about her daily goings-on even though she felt in doing so she was ridiculous, and, to his face, she had made a point of praising his plumage and acumen. Surely his hostility had waned.

Alas, no. His first act of freedom had been to chomp the cartilage of her ear. She was aghast at his malice and fled, shutting the dining room door behind her. Soon, however, her insult at the profound ingratitude of a bird that bit the hand that fed it was replaced by anger as she listened to the rending sounds of Tiko redecorating her dining room. And then, decent person that she is, she became worried. She heard him bouncing off the walls, hurtling around the room in a kind of frenetic frenzy. It was Hitchcock all over again: the mad beating of wings, the flailing feathers, the special intensity in the panic of the flitting, fluttering world. Tiko's fury continued unabated as we stood helplessly by the door.

"Why?" Josie was visibly shaken.

"He's out of control," I said. "Overexcited. And he's not familiar with the room."

"What should we do?"

"Not much we can do. He's too agitated."

"Won't he hurt himself?"

"No. He'll be fine." I thought of a pet gull I'd once had who flew through my house and knocked a tire onto himself. He was so traumatized that he lost his voice for two months, but was otherwise unharmed. I decided to keep the story to myself.

Gradually, the room quieted. Before I left I flipped the light switch off, which was fortunately outside the dining room door. Josie called later that evening to say that sometime around nightfall Tiko had returned to his cage. In the darkness she had tiptoed in and locked the cage door. That was the end of Tiko's flights around her house.

In the days that followed, I stopped by to find him passing the time walking in a tight little circle along his perch, up the side of his cage, and, hanging upside down, across the bars of the roof. Using his claws and his beak, he climbed with great agility. He varied his speeds, sometimes walking so rapidly that the clicking sounds reminded me of an approaching train. At other times his pace was excruciatingly slow: he almost seemed to have forgotten what he was doing. When he wasn't pacing, he stared into space.

I watched his endless circuits, mesmerized. This pacing, a nervous habit of many captive animals, begins as an antidote to boredom but can develop into a psychotic act. If and when the animal is freed or has a change in its environment (a larger cage, a companion, or the introduction of toys to play with), it regains its sanity.

Spring came and he molted, the once bright red feathers on his forehead giving way to dull orange ones. The bluish sheen vanished from his head, and some of the brilliant green feathers were replaced by plumes of olive gray. His lackluster color was a sure sign that he was undernourished. In Florida, where he'd dined like a sultan, the requisite food groups took care of themselves; now, whether out of spite or the depression that had overwhelmed his disposition, he ignored Josie's offerings. He seemed to be on a protracted hunger strike against the injustices visited upon him by the world. In some strange way he seemed to be punishing Josie for the loss of his two companions and his Florida home.

He began to move around the cage less often, and his droppings accumulated in a heap. He huddled silently with drooping wings, his feathers fluffed, his head withdrawn. He ceased to look around. In the mornings he still called a bit, but more softly, for briefer periods. It was as if he anticipated being shrouded in darkness, for, understandably, Josie covered his cage to calm and quiet him when he persisted in his anguished shrieks.

Tiko, in all this, was far from unique. Parrots are intensely social: deprived of company, they will exhibit acute symptoms of depression, not unlike human beings. They stop eating, cease to play, and become hostile and withdrawn. Their feathers turn lifeless and dull. Prolonged depression leads to stress, which can result in ceaseless preening to the point where some birds pull out enough feathers to expose their skin. Some may pluck feathers from just one part of the body, while others will strip themselves naked. Parrots hate change. In certain birds even a small variation in diet or routine, even a new cage, can trigger obsessive preening. Some parrots, it is true, grow angry rather than depressed or stressed, and some others are able to go with the flow.

People familiar with parrots will understand that it is next to impossible not to develop a sense of what they think and feel. This presents behaviorists (of which I am one) with a dilemma. Our training drills into us an aversion to anthropomorphic judgments. I once considered it the epitome of bad science to attribute human thought, feelings, and language ability to animals. But over the years I have changed my mind. I have come to regard it as at least equally benighted to automatically assume that animals lack these qualities. I find myself amazed, in fact, that anyone could doubt that the animals closest to us—dogs, cats, horses, parrots (especially parrots)—have emotional responses to the things around them, or that anyone could question the proposition that they form ideas about the situations they find themselves in or the people they meet. Over time, I gave in to my growing conviction that the thoughts and feelings of certain animals can be read from their behavior. A number of scientists will doubtless regard this as anthropomorphic, the height of sloppy thinking and pseudo-science, but no one who has lived with a parrot will for a second doubt that they have thoughts and feelings similar to ours.

Although we, especially in this culture, like to see ourselves as autonomous individuals, the social fabric is woven deep in our being. I don't know which came first for me, this intuitive understanding of what it means to be human or my research over the past two decades, much of which has made it clear to me that social behavior plays a vital role in the lives of animals, contributing to their survival and to their happiness. They are like us. Their sense of themselves, their identity, is, in large part, determined by the group. Nowhere is this clearer than in parrots. Tiko has been my greatest teacher in this regard. As we will see, I have observed in him behavior in our Somerset home that mirrors precisely what I've observed in parrots in the wild. His courting of me is only one example and is part of a large picture of the way parrots organize themselves. Their relationships are stable and long-term. They live in flocks, with tightly bonded extended families that remain together for years. They are monogamous throughout their long lives, which in captivity can be as long as sixty or seventy years. For much of the time, they remain with their mates twenty-four hours a day. Reproductive duties may occasionally separate them: the male goes off to find a nest; one partner incubates the eggs while the other goes to feed. A mated pair will take turns leaving the nest to find food for their young. Apart from this, they are always together.

Lifelong monogamy is not uncommon among birds; it is practiced by geese, herons, ibises, and most seabirds (divorce does occasionally occur when a pair is unsuccessful in raising young). I find it touching that these birds, like parrots, develop long-term, monogamous relationships to a much greater extent than do, say, chimps, baboons, gorillas. In this sense, studying parrots, and the many other birds that mate for life, tells us more about ourselves than studying primates.

Over the course of any one breeding season, fully 90 percent of all bird species are monogamous. But because small birds live only two or three years, they often lose their mate after one breeding season and are forced to find another.

Aside from a certain sentimental value that we like to attach to monogamy, there is a great evolutionary advantage in mating for life, and this is clearly the case with long-lived birds. A mated pair entering a breeding season is far more likely to raise young successfully than birds who have to search for a mate. Paired birds do not have to expend time and energy courting, so they can breed earlier in the season, which, as I've said, gives their young more time to gain weight before the winter or dry season comes, or it's time to fly south for the winter. Birds in the habit of raising young together have already worked out the details of parenting: how much time each will spend incubating eggs; the frequency with which each goes off to forage for food for their young. I've often wondered how parrots decide which shift one or the other will take. How do human couples decide who puts the kids to bed or comforts a sick child in the middle of the night? Parrot pairs also make these decisions. There are no gender roles in the raising of young, and each pair must work out its own rhythm, which takes some time to perfect and gives the advantage to established couples. It is perhaps worth pointing out that the evolutionary advantage of mating for life has held true for most of human evolution as well. Raising a child was not possible alone; it took two. A single parent couldn't manage, and even today single parents struggle with the burden and responsibility of raising a child alone.

TIKO MAY HAVE BONDED more strongly with Libby because Freda teased him—and parrots do not take kindly to teasing. But when the chilly winds of November stripped the last leaves from the trees and the cold set in, Libby declined quickly, and she died in 1986. Tiko's last link to Florida was gone. He remained solitary in his cage, unable to fathom why his loved ones did not return. My heart went out to him; I yearned to make a move in his direction, but I knew he would resent the overture if I disappeared soon after making it, and he might never trust me again.

Shortly after Libby's funeral, Josie called to say that Tiko was ours, if we wanted him. While saddened by Libby's death, I had found it painful to watch the bird deteriorate, and was relieved that his ordeal was over. For the first time, though, it occurred to me that he might be too ill to recover. And I wondered if he would be able to transfer his affection to Mike and me, and adjust to yet another environment.

Still, there was no question in my mind that we should take him. We spent several days parrot-proofing our house, and making it as junglelike as possible. We bought a rhododendron and a fig tree. We built perches and we cleared surfaces. We moved unstable objects to the floor. At last we were ready. We thought it would be easier on Tiko if I went alone to pick him up—parrots usually respond better to women than to men—and so I went next door heady with anticipation.

I could approach Tiko with a different attitude. He would be coming home with me, for good. Josie was similarly relieved; she knew the bird needed the love and attention she was unable to give him. And, of course, she wanted him out of her house.

I took a seat near his cage, placing my finger at the edge of the bars, within his reach.

"Better not do that," Josie said. "He will bite, and believe me, he can take a chunk out."

I ignored the warning. "Tiko, sweetie," I crooned. "I've come to take you home."

He raced toward me across his wooden perch. I resisted the urge to move my finger. Josie cringed.

But I knew that this first contact was critical. Despite the chance of injury, I had to appear vulnerable. If he took a dislike to me now, he might never change his mind.

He halted inches from my finger and peered into my eyes; neither of us moved. "Pretty parrot, pretty Tiko," I murmured. "We're going to be friends." The seconds ticked by, and I kept talking. "You'll have a good home with us, sweetie. You can fly free. You'll love our house. Don't be afraid. Come, Tiko, come see me."

With the bars separating us, he had to come to me, or scurry to the other side of the cage, should that be his choice. My task was to be available, to let him choose.

He turned slowly toward my finger, his bill very close. He lunged. But instead of biting me he bent his head until his beak touched the perch. His neck feathers rose. Josie giggled in relief. I realized my own heart had been racing. I had been tested; when I hadn't pulled away, his aggression turned to something else. He'd made the first move, exposed his vulnerable neck to me. And now he waited.

I extended my finger and carefully began to scratch his head and neck, still murmuring to him. He called so softly that I barely heard him, but I knew that things were going to be all right.

"Amazing," Josie said. "He used to let my mother scratch his neck, but I never thought I'd see it happen again."

The parrot sidled closer. He pressed against the bars of the cage and lowered his head. I gently caressed his neck, feeling his vulnerability, knowing what was happening—the beginning of my commitment to a creature that might live on for another fifty years. He called again, still very softly, and moved to the center of the cage. I had at last introduced myself, and, starved for affection as he was, he'd let me into his world. I slowly covered his cage with the blanket I'd brought for the purpose, all the while gently explaining things to him. "It's time to go home, Tiko. You're coming to our house for good. I'm covering your cage to protect you from the wind. We're not going far."

He didn't understand a word, of course, but he knew from my tone that all was well. We edged down the steps and through the snow. It was bitterly cold, with a gusty wind. The snow was several inches deep, the path slippery. But I spoke to him the whole way. "You're all right, Tiko. Hang on to your perch, we're almost there." He emitted one short, tentative call, then fell silent. Cradling my precious cargo, I negotiated the icy stairs leading to our door.

3

A Parrot in the House

I MADE A BEELINE FOR OUR OFFICE, STILL WEARING MY coat, the cage wrapped in my arms. Mike scaled the stairs behind me.

"How did he seem?"

"Okay," I said over my shoulder. "He let me put my finger in his cage."

I was winded by the time bird and cage came to rest on the stand Mike and I had set up for Tiko, in the office we shared on the top floor of the house. The moment of truth had arrived—the great unveiling! Warbling sweet nothings, I slowly, like a magician, plucked the blanket off the roost. There stood the parrot, a noble creature blinking in the flood of winter sunlight angling in over the bare trees through the room's large south-facing picture window.

He blinked several times, pupils constricting, then took a quick look around. The office sprawls across the entire top floor of our redbrick house. It's large enough to hold a bed, four desks, hundreds of books, banks of filing cabinets, numerous tables piled high with the paper trail of two scientists who are rarely at work on fewer than five or six projects at a time, and knickknacks we've collected from around the world: a green stone carving of a puffin from a graduate student; a mask made by my brother Roy when he was eight; stuffed animals and birds; a parrot mobile; blown glass from Murano, Italy; arrowheads I found on my parents' farm when my brother Mel, my sister Tina, and I picked tomatoes; a wooden crocodile mask; an Audubon print of grackles eating corn (which reminds me of my childhood). This was to be Tiko's home. (He would eventually move into Debbie's room, after she went off to graduate school. Debbie and David lived mostly with their mother, Mike's first wife, and stayed with us on weekends and holidays; but when Tiko became part of our family, David was a teenager with an active social life, and Debbie was already off at college. Consequently, they weren't much around.) We had decided that the office, where we spent so much of our time, would be the best place for Tiko's cage—he could return to its familiar, protective environment and still have the two of us nearby.

Tiko scanned his new digs while Mike and I stood a discreet distance away, talking to him in dulcet tones and beaming like proud parents. I needed to establish a way whereby Tiko could let us know when he was ready to leave his cage. Once again I placed my fingertip between the cage's bars. If he lunged, or bit me, I would know he was in no hurry to go anywhere. Behind me, I could feel Mike inwardly flinch, but he stood perfectly still and didn't make a sound. I watched Tiko closely for any indication that he was registering Mike's mood, but he seemed to have missed it. He was intent on studying the out-landish human digit that had the effrontery to invade his sanctuary. He walked across his perch, seemed poised to strike, and then his wings fanned slightly outward like an umbrella beginning to open, his head drooped down, and he began to nibble very gently on my finger with the deadly pincer of his beak that had struck such terror in Josie's heart. The shrieking harpy of the skies had become as gentle as a lamb.

Mike applauded lightly as I took in the sensation of the hard probe of his tongue outlining the contours of my fingernail and his beak moving ever so lightly on my skin. We kept this pose for a long, silent minute. There was nothing precarious about it, nothing tenu-ous; he seemed all there, in no hurry, and then I gently pulled my fin-ger away, took off my coat and hat, and let another moment pass before I opened the cage door and slid in my hand. With no hesitation he climbed onto my upturned fingers, and I carried him to a free-standing perch, two dowels affixed at right angles, that we had set up for him on a small wooden table. At one end of the horizontal dowel we'd attached a flat, square platform for his food dish, which we had stocked with Cheerios, fresh strawberries, bits of apple, lettuce, and carrots. As if studying an unfamiliar menu, he contemplated the array. Then he attacked the strawberries, leaving just a single slice; he tossed a lettuce leaf into the air, pecking at it savagely when it hap-pened to land back on the tray. He sampled the carrots, put away most of the apple. The Cheerios, which at first he had regarded some-what balefully, he now lifted in his claw, one by one, and carefully consumed. He appeared to regard them as dessert. After six months of Josie's parrot mix, he had clearly been ready for a hearty meal.

For the rest of that first evening Mike and I worked away at a joint project, the final chapters of a book we were coauthoring on the Common Tern. Tiko regarded us from his perch. We took pains not to direct too much attention his way, considering it the wiser course to let him adjust at his own pace to new people and new surroundings. When it was time to turn in, I presented him with a stick, as Libby and Freda had done for all those years in Florida. He climbed on without ado, and I ferried him across the room and into his cage. He grasped its perch with his beak and then with the long powerful toes (two in front and two behind) of one foot and then the other. He straightened and regarded me with a direct, unblinking gaze. This is where he would sleep, upright, his toes locked tightly around the dowel, his head sunk deep into the soft, powdery feathers of his neck, the thin saurian lids of his eyes barely closed, ready, in the way of wild things, to take flight at a moment's notice.

"Sleep well, Tiko sweetheart. We'll see you in the morning."

He stood unmoving, gazing at my face. It was unlikely he would leave his cage during the night, but I shut the door nonetheless. No need to risk his wandering about and injuring himself in unfamiliar surroundings. He didn't move, which I took to mean he was content. Pacing would signal distress or discomfort.

Mike and I settled into bed downstairs, pleased by our newly minted threesome. The dark quiet house felt different, inhabited as it was by a strange new spirit, a jungle sprite. There was a faint click as Mike turned out the light. The ghostly electric glow of the neighborhood seeped around the corners of the curtains, creating a pale orange luminance in the room. The streets were quiet, but somewhere, far away in the distance, I could hear the sound of the cars speeding along the distant highway; trucks barreled through the night. Mike's breathing became deep and slow. But my mind, left alone with itself, whirled on in the darkness.

Had I really known, when I went after Tiko, what I was taking on? How would he like living with two preoccupied, busy academics and adjusting to their absurd schedules—the teaching, the research, the often extended absences on field trips? He had spent the last six months without diversion, without the chance to fly free. By now he must be fairly crotchety himself. He was a middle-aged parrot who might turn out not to like me very much, and he might hang around in that frame of mind for fifty years. I drew a deep breath. Even if it took the rest of our lives, I resolved, I would earn his trust. And with that resolution I felt myself relax.

I was startled from sleep the next morning by a single, piercing parrot squawk. Mike, as usual, had been up for hours, and was puttering about downstairs in the kitchen. I groggily climbed the stairs to the office and put my finger within Tiko's reach. He nibbled at it. He seemed all at once eager to leave his cage.

It was to be our first full day together, a Saturday; I had picked Tiko up on a Friday so we could keep an eye on him all weekend. He sat on his perch by Mike's desk—a narrow maple limb attached to a lamp stand. He took in the objects in his purview, simultaneously keeping one eye on Mike and the other on me as we worked across the room from each other. I found his scrutiny somehow comforting. Occasionally he closed his eyes, or tucked his head into his back feathers and dozed. He seemed unperturbed when either Mike or I briefly left the room, but on one thoughtless occasion, when we took a break together, he squawked, glided down from his perch, and came waddling across the floor in pursuit. His long claws caught in the carpet and he almost fell. But he righted himself, and clomped after us.

His legs were quite far apart when he walked, and he seemed pigeon-toed, yet he could move with surprising speed. It was impossible to determine whether he feared being left alone or was impelled by curiosity, but whenever we entered a new room he carefully walked its perimeter as if measuring the square footage, climbing over whatever might stand in his way, peering behind each piece of furniture as if looking for a place to hide or roost. We gave him the grand tour, then trooped back upstairs.

When it was time for lunch I got up again from the bed. I've never done well at a desk, due to my short stature and a curvature of the spine, but I was quite comfortable on a bed. With a pillow wedged behind me, and my legs extended, I could work for long periods.

My grumbling stomach told me it was lunchtime, and I looked up from my work. "Mike, Tiko, let's eat."

Tiko seemed at once to understand this suggestion, for he opened his wings, pushing off from his perch as if to take to the sky. Instead, he plummeted to the rug in a flurry of feathers and claws. It appeared he had forgotten how to fly. It was an awful moment. He glanced at me quickly then lowered his head, pulling his feathers tightly against his body, seeming to shrink before me. His posture bespoke mortification. He seemed somehow diminished in his own eyes, a fallen thing. My heart went out to him, and I looked away, not wanting to prolong his humiliation. His flight muscles had atrophied after months in a cage, much like the leg muscles of a patient confined to bed rest. The flight muscles in birds aren't in their wings, as you might assume. Instead they form the mass of breast muscle anchored to the breastbone, or sternum, and its large keel. From there it is mainly tendons that extend into the wing, attached to the strong but light humerus and wrist bones. Given time and practice, Tiko's muscles would grow strong again, just so long as he didn't stop trying. I fervently hoped that he hadn't been so startled by this first failed attempt that he'd refuse to try to fly again. The possibility was heartrending—I knew it was vitally important for his sense of self to be able to move one day through the house with the same ease and grace as his forebears and his wild coevals flew through Central America's tropical forests.

"It's okay, Tiko," I said. "One thing at a time." We decided to risk leaving him there, and descended to the dining room. He did not follow. When we returned, after a pensive lunch, he had made his way back to his perch, climbing up a wooden ladder to reach it, and, ignoring our entry, was savoring a Cheerio.

I CANCELED ALL my meetings and office hours that week, coming straight home after teaching. I was at a point in my academic career where I was allowed some liberties, eccentricities even, although I took no special pains to explain to anyone the reason for my absence from the hallowed halls of academe. I didn't miss my duties. I could work at home, and Tiko completely preoccupied me. We quickly developed a comfortable routine. I worked on the office bed; he could approach me as he pleased, be in or out of his cage as he chose. I was able to work and chatter at him at the same time—"Everything okay, Tiko? You're welcome next to me anytime"—so that he'd grow accustomed to my voice. Once, he waddled to the bed and tried to scale the covers. But the sleek surface of the bedspread bedeviled him: he found no purchase, and slid repeatedly to the floor. After I covered the bedspread with an afghan, which had plenty of beak- and toe-holds, he was able to scale the bed's sheer face like a mountaineer. He would park himself six inches away from me on a pile of papers. He vocalized from time to time. He seemed to be talking in flowing syntactical phrases, his own parrot grammar, perhaps the garbled pidgin Yiddish Josie had mentioned. Once I thought I heard him say, "Gimme a cracker," but he had waddled off toward his food perch before I could respond. He also said "No!" quite clearly when he didn't want a bit of food, and "Hello" sometimes when I entered the room.

We plied him with a daily assortment of fruits and vegetables, eager to see him replenish the nutrients he'd lost. He never refused to eat, which pleased us, but we soon observed an oddity: he'd consume one food only for three or four days—lettuce, say, or melon—then abandon it utterly and switch to carrots, or apples. What the devil was he up to? Unfortunately, the food he didn't eat he didn't simply ignore—he tended first to play with it, then toss it to the floor. Parrots in the wild also are sloppy eaters. But Tiko tossed his food with such zeal that Mike and I thought that perhaps something else was going on—maybe it was, for parrots, the "terrible thirties"?

As biologists, we understood that so far as Tiko was concerned, we had entered *his* world, not the other way round. People acquire pets, but pets wind up dealing with people——captive in our homes, forced to interact with us on our schedules, not theirs. The cat demolishing your couch is not being "bad," nor commenting unfavorably on your living room decor. She needs to trim and sharpen her claws, which are constantly growing. All you need do is buy her a scratching post and she'll leave the furniture alone. Much as we do when we study animals in the field, Mike and I strove to see the world from Tiko's perspective. We tried to uncover his motivations, ease our way into a bird's-eye view. Our suburban home had become, in a sense, the wild tropical forest of Tiko's ancestors, the pair of us pressed into service as the flock of his generational memory. We began to be inducted, during this first period, into Tiko's complex feeding and flocking behaviors. More and deeper inductions would follow.

THESE FIRST MONTHS with Tiko were an amazing experience. He was incredibly curious about the things we did. He explored every nook in every room. I'd never had a bird become fully integrated into my household, and I began to see the scientific possibilities of observing Tiko's behavior over a long period of time in an environment where he felt completely at home. For example, wherever I've had the opportunity to observe parrots——in Brazil's Amazon rain forest, around Tikal in Guatemala, on Mexico's Yucatán Peninsula——I've been struck by their flocking behavior. When any one member decides to leave a roosting tree, the entire flock departs, skimming the treetops, calling loudly to keep themselves together. Tiko, from the very first day in our house, did the same thing. He would sit quietly with Mike and me, his flock, until we left for another room. Then he would be galvanized into action, climbing to the floor and waddling in our wake.

But there were complications. One morning, when I left the office, Tiko did not follow me out. "I'm leaving now," I told him. He blinked at me from his perch. "What's up? You're not coming?" I watched him wipe his bill with some force on the perch, raise one foot with an opened claw, and click his beak, usually an indication in parrots of nervousness or a change in mood. But I was thinking about breakfast, and I was running late. What was the bird's problem? Left alone, I was afraid he'd hurt himself. Exasperated, I walked back and presented him my hand. He regarded it with menace, hackles rising, irises constricted. He emitted a short, rankled squawk, then lunged.

"Don't you *dare* snap at me, Tiko. Hop on, we've got to go."

Then, quick as a cobra, he struck, the sharp beak chomping down on my index finger. I was, at first, amazed at his speed and taken aback by his wrath; then incensed because I was late; then dismayed because I didn't want to leave him while he was angry at me. The two punctures bled. They were, fortunately, shallow and close together, which made it clear to me that he was only slightly miffed. What all parrots have in common, and what distinguishes them from most other birds, is their formidable beak (the curved upper mandible fits snugly over the lower one) and highly developed jaw muscles, which can crack open the toughest nut. (Hawks and parrots share this strong, hooked bill.) Had Tiko been really ticked off, the sharp tips of his upper and lower bills would have inflicted considerably more damage.

———

TIKO WAS OFTEN in a foul mood in those early days, lunging and squawking, nipping and biting, and I, confronted by an ornery bird, was often out of sorts as well. He gave only a brief warning before he bit, and it took me a little longer than perhaps it should have to read all the signs. A forward lunge or an extended neck were clear warnings to keep my distance. And since Tiko was often ambivalent, his messages were ambiguous, and I frequently misunderstood them.

Our skirmishes typically erupted when he wanted something that I knew he shouldn't have (he liked chewing on pencils, for example, which contained not only lead but toxic cadmium in the yellow paint) or refused to go somewhere I needed him to go. I'd try to snatch the pencil away but he'd hang on to his end. A tug of war would ensue, with me trying to reason with him about the dangers of pencils and him yanking on the pencil and giving me the evil eye. I eventually learned to distract him with a pinyon nut, which was perhaps the point of it all. Early on in the relationship I could never have guessed that he was subtly training me, but in retrospect the subversive pattern is clear. When I couldn't simply talk him into following me I'd present him with the stick, which he would utterly ignore, or lunge at, or climb onto and bite fiercely. His will was intense—he wanted what he wanted when he wanted it, and the converse as well.

Most people in this part of the world prefer their pets docile and well-behaved, and it is interesting to speculate why this should be so. Does owning a pliable pet create in people the illusion of control, at least over a portion of our lives? Such a creature provides unconditional love and devotion. It doesn't talk back or disagree; if it behaves "well," you may reward it, in your wisdom, with love. I've always preferred pets, however, that retained a wild streak, that did not feel obliged to bend to my will.

Intellectually, too, I understood that Tiko wasn't being "disobedient"; he was simply being what he was: a parrot. So it came as something of a shock to find that the bird, from time to time, got my blood boiling. Particularly irksome was his refusal to accompany me when I left one room for another. I have already mentioned flocking behavior, but even in the wild one or two maverick parrots will sometimes tarry. Still, I found it disconcerting that Tiko would behave this way in our house. Was he fearful? Or was the fear all mine? Perhaps I was overly concerned that he might hurt himself if left alone. Was I being too much of a mother hen? Was I confining him, constricting him? Was he rebelling against an irksome parental authority? Whatever it was, Tiko appeared to regard my efforts to move him as a battle of wills, and I'm not sure he was wrong.

Despite my determination, in those early days, to respect his autonomy, I may well have confounded my own needs with his. It could have been that I wanted him to tag along not from fear that he might hurt himself if left alone, but for the pleasure of his company. And once he made it plain he was not much interested in my society, perhaps it became a question of no more than getting him to do what I wanted him to do.

Even though it's now cliché, I think it's true that we assume we're superior to the rest of the animal kingdom, what the Book of Genesis calls man's "dominion over the fish of the sea, and over the fowl of the air, and cattle after their kind, and everything that creepeth upon the earth . . ." We're all susceptible to this notion. Many of the contrary attitudes I run into while doing conservation work have their roots in the almost unconscious assumption that human beings are destined to exercise control over the natural world.

Growing up on a farm did provide me with some resistance to this point of view. We struggled to dominate nature, yet never came close. Hawks, owls, and foxes wreaked havoc on my dad's five thousand chickens. Floods and hail destroyed our crops. Several weeks of ill-timed drought could ruin a harvest. And always, birds ate away at what was left. My scientific training, too, chipped away at the idea of man's superiority. Evolution teaches us that everything alive today is as equally well adapted and performs as well as humans do. Yet despite my background in science, my love of animals, and my early lessons on the farm, the concept of man's dominance is so ingrained in us that it fell to Tiko to eliminate all such vestiges in me. He went to work at once, but it did not happen right away.

While I was still laboring under the misguided notion that I was the boss, I tried to discipline Tiko for his hostile behavior. But it's just not possible to punish a parrot. They do not grow meek in the face of anger, do not respond to censure with contrition. They match you blow for blow. I was obliged to remind myself that although Tiko had been born in captivity, he was only a generation removed from the wild. Though humans have kept parrots as pets for centuries, there is no history of their domestication, as there is with cats and dogs. Throughout history it's been easier and cheaper for people to find parrots in the wild than to breed them in captivity. This ineradicable wildness, even in captive-bred birds, is part of their fascination; it makes the tight bonds they form with people all the more remarkable. But in those early days I often found myself thinking wistfully of Tiko's bond with Libby and Freda, and harboring doubts that the three of us would ever achieve such closeness.

ON WEEKENDS, or whenever I knew I'd be spending an extended period of time at home, I wore glasses to protect my eyes, long-sleeved shirts to shield my arms, and I tried to remember to make sure that my hair covered my ears. It seemed the better part of valor, where Tiko was concerned, to spare him temptation. He never did attack my eyes, but the potential for serious damage was such that I saw no point in taking chances. He did go for our ears, especially mine, since he spent so much time on my shoulders. He'd ride around up there, and our ideas of when it was time to dismount did not always coincide. I'd bring him to his perch and lean toward it, but in a certain frame of mind he'd dig in his claws, squawk or curse at me in what I assumed was his garbled Yiddish, and start pecking at my ear. I'd be forced to present him with his stick, onto which he would, usually, begrudgingly climb, biting it instead of me. Those nips on the earlobe did not, fortunately, leave scars, the way the bites on the forearm did.

I wondered if he was not acting maliciously. When he punctured my skin, he also punctured the veil of my scientific detachment. Mike and I had early on assumed that his hostility came from his having been thrust into a new environment; his distress from the new, dependent relationship with us over which he had no control. We both felt that his hostility and distress were heightened by his inability to fly. Still, we'd been paragons of calm consistency and understanding over those first few months, and our attitude was unchanged. I might be teaching a class or working on a chapter of a book, or deeply involved (I thought) in reading, when I would discover that what I had really been focused on was what there still remained to do to salvage the stormy relationship I had with what I still thought of as "our" bird.

But I never feared him, and this went a long way toward eventual détente. Once some animals sense your fear, their aggression grows. Experiments have shown that people emit "fear pheromones," and that a dog can smell them. While a parrot lacks a dog's olfactory sense, its vision is keen enough to identify fear on the basis, say, of tentative movements, a subtle backing away, a drawing of the hands or head in toward the body. I fearlessly clung to the belief that if Mike and I were consistent with Tiko, if he got it through his head that we weren't going to go away, he would eventually adapt.

And it wasn't such an effort to keep my heart open to him. Even during the difficult early days he often filled me with joy. Being a biologist never ceases to provide me with the sense of wonder and discovery I had as I child for the world around me. Tiko was my link to the wildness of our planet, to the forests of his forebears, to the creatures that had captured my imagination as a girl. Sometimes I'd look over at him and be awed by his spunk, his profound curiosity. But the sense of wonder was being constantly tainted, even eroded, by his fearsome beak, the scars I still bear on both my arms.

———

IN THE FARM CULTURE where I grew up, the adage that the way to a man's heart is through his stomach was taken as a matter of course; sharing meals is a foundation of family and community in cultures all over the world. So, too, for Tiko. The way to the bird's heart seemed to be through his belly.

He loved nuts and chocolate. He knew where Mike hid the Hershey's Kisses and the M&M's. When he was given these he'd gloat and shower us with cheeps, trills, and fetching squawks. Whenever we were in the kitchen, he'd walk over to the cabinet that contained the goodies and peck its door. He'd peck the nut jar's lid as well. If Mike and I remained unmoved, he'd run a yard in each direction, then cock his head at us. How could we fail to see what he wanted?

We discovered that his hearing—through ears the diameter of a pencil, hidden by feathers just behind his eyes—was preternaturally sharp. He could hear Mike unwrap the foil on a chocolate Kiss from several rooms away. Mike would be startled by the sound of claws clicking at a smart pace down the hall, and Tiko would charge into the kitchen. Mike would usually oblige him and give him a Kiss. Using his tongue and lower bill, Tiko could strip away the foil in seconds, much as he husked nuts. But one Kiss would merely whet his appetite. He'd look up at Mike and mew.

He also had a weakness for M&M's, stripping off the colored sugar coating to get at the chocolate within. (I later learned that parrots in the wild strip the paper-thin coat off seeds because it has higher levels of toxins called tannins.) We tried to ration his intake, since too much chocolate is bad for birds (bad for humans, too, but I have even less control over what Mike eats). Tiko would lunge, his all-purpose response to not getting what he wanted. When that strategy failed, he'd sulk in a corner and ignore us. If we left the room and he waddled behind us, now out of visual range of the coveted object, all was forgotten and forgiven. If, on the other hand, we were obliged to remain where we were, in order to cook dinner, say, these sulks could become interminable.

I NEVER TIRED OF WATCHING the small ways in which Tiko adapted to his new environment. He devised a brilliant method for descending the stairs, which was more difficult for him than climbing them. He'd stand with his feet at the edge of the top landing and lower his bill until it touched the stair below. Although it was a considerable reach, he'd bring his right foot down to where his bill was resting. There he'd be, his bill and right foot on the stair below, his left foot still buried in the carpet of the stair above. He reminded me of someone with one foot in a rowboat and one foot on the shore. It appeared that he would never get himself righted, but it crossed my mind that parrots, along with woodpeckers, are the only birds with zygodactyl feet (two toes pointing forward, two to the rear), which permit them to grasp branches, climb with great agility, and manipulate objects with ease. Nevertheless it struck me as a leap of faith when he detached his left claw and let his body plop forward onto the stair below, supported mainly by his bill. As awkward as it looked, he would eventually be able to whip down a flight of stairs almost as rapidly as I could walk them.

Although he still couldn't fly, he learned that he could glide, just so long as his destination was lower than his launchpad. He became expert at gliding from his perches to the floor, or from the top of the fridge to the table where we often placed him. After several weeks of practice strengthening his flight muscles, he became strong enough to make the journey between two destinations on the same plane.

I was in the kitchen one afternoon pouring myself a glass of juice when Tiko sauntered in. He announced his wish to be carried to the counter by giving a low croon and pecking gently at my toes, but my hands were full. "Hang on a minute, love," I told him. He stopped pecking and seemed to ponder my request. He must have grown tired of waiting, because, flapping furiously, he pushed up off the floor. I feared he wouldn't make it, but he landed right beside the carton of juice, panting. He looked around and fluffed his feathers out. "Superb, Tiko!" I said. He fixed me with a steady gaze, then did a prideful strut around the carton.

For quite a while a few feet was all he could manage, and he'd reach his destination worn out and breathing hard; but he was clearly on his way. I no longer had to worry that he'd chicken out. I could now look forward to the day that I'd see him flying proudly through the house.

DURING THOSE EARLY DAYS, Tiko seemed uncertain whether to bond with Mike, or me, or take on the pair of us. He ambivalently solicited us both. He would lower his head as if to request preening, but when either of us began to scratch his neck he'd lift his head aggressively and lunge, or else pull away with a short, raucous squawk. Seconds later, the sequence would be repeated.

He was sometimes ill-tempered with company. Our Red-lored Amazon turned into the Red Baron. There was no way to predict who would invoke his wrath. He favored females, but not always. He was never happy to see my sister Tina. A sisterly hug provoked an attack, thankfully on me, not her. He seemed jealous of my affection for her, and took his anger out by nipping at my hand or ear and flying at me wildly. He followed his attacks by flying to my shoulder to preen my hair, his way of saying, "I didn't mean it," or "I'm so cute you can't possibly dislike me."

On the other hand, he took instantly to Mike's mother, Anne. In her gentle way, Anne would sit back and wait, making quiet conversation with us, ignoring Tiko completely. This pleased him. Although her hair is short—not Tiko's usual preference—he managed to find a strand here or there to delicately preen. She knows Yiddish and tried to interpret his squawks and warblings, but to no avail. Perhaps he was losing the little bit of the language he knew, now that he wasn't around Josie's mother and aunt? Mike's father, Alex, in his jovial, humorous way, would approach Tiko immediately upon entering the house, kibitzing with him, trying to draw him out. He was always summarily rebuffed. The same preference held true when the telephone was on speaker. To Anne, Tiko happily cooed; Alex elicited silence.

There was a similar problem with Guy Tudor, a MacArthur fellow, and Michelle LeMarchant, two of our oldest friends. One look at Michelle (who'd owned toucans for years) and Tiko was smitten. But for Guy, a renowned artist who specializes in drawing and painting birds, Tiko held a peculiar contempt. Guy was hurt. "This bird is neurotic," he often said to me. He tried to make friends by offering Tiko goodies, all of which, even chocolate, Tiko refused.

There was one consistency in Tiko's like and dislikes: he had a weakness for children. But he liked them best when they were small. As my nephews Jacob and Daniel grew taller, he switched his allegiances to Erik, Douglass, and Ben, and then to Beth, Emily, and Andy. Whenever kids were around, he wanted to be on their shoulder or knee. Theodore Roosevelt had a Hyacinth Macaw that shared this trait. The macaw climbed over children who came to the White House with delicacy and care, a frightening experience for the uninitiated. The Hyacinth is an eagle-sized bird whose bill, as Roosevelt liked to remark, can cut through boilerplate.

WHEN NOT OPENLY HOSTILE to us, Tiko was often remote. This did not really surprise me. As with any new relationship, there were things to work out, understandings to be forged. I had known from the start what I was in for, so it was not as if his moodiness and chronic hostility took me completely by surprise. If parrots lived exclusively with human beings, they would respond to us differently. We usually breed adverse traits out of animals. The wild ancestors of cows in India are actually quite aggressive, but we have bred the beasts into Jerseys and Holsteins. Likewise, we could breed parrots to fetch us our slippers and sing us lullabies.

Even though Tiko has spent his whole life in captivity, he is not domesticated. His temperament reflects many of the 353 species of parrots living in the wild, which range in size from the four-inch-long Buff-faced Pygmy Parrot of New Guinea to the forty-inch Hyacinth Macaw of Brazil, with its four-foot wingspan. Tiko is about thirteen inches long, typical of an Amazon, much larger than cockatiels and budgies, which are also parrots. So, too, are parrotlets, parakeets, lories and lorikeets, African and Asian lovebirds, cockatoos, conures, and New Zealand Keas and Kakapos.

Although many species of parrots may occasionally forage on the ground, particularly in Australia, only three are strictly ground dwellers. There are only two nocturnal parrots, and both are endangered (the Owl Parrot, or Kakapo, of New Zealand, and the Australian Ground Parrot). The Kakapo is the heaviest parrot in the world; the average adult weighs eight and a half pounds (Tiko is less than a pound). It is unable to fly, but uses its well-developed wings in courtship and to break its fall when it glides down from the trees it climbs. The Kakapo is also unusual in that it is mostly solitary, except during courtship, when its deep booming voice echoes over the moors where the last few members of its species survive.

Parrots are mainly vegetarians—many smaller species eat seeds or fruits, while lorikeets have evolved long, tapering bills to access the pollen and nectar of trumpet flowers, eucalyptus, and melaleuca. Parrots also dine on nuts, pollen, roots, lichens, leaves, and bark. Less common are flesh-eating species, such as the Kaka of New Zealand, which eats mainly insects and insect larvae. Then there is the true carnivore, the rather drab olive-green Kea, which lives in the snow-capped mountains of New Zealand. (Keas, interestingly enough, are also the only polygamous parrots.) The Kea stands accused of killing sheep in order to reach the fatty covering over their kidneys. When I was in New Zealand, several sheep farmers told me they have watched Kea land on the back of sheep and peck vigorously through the fleece and flanks until they reached the kidneys. Some Keas pick the eyes from lambs. Keas have been persecuted unmercifully for this unpopular habit. This is a bum rap because only an occasional rogue Kea dines on sheep. Fortunately, sheep were scarce in Somerset, and, in any event, Tiko has not shown a fondness for mutton.

PARROTS ARE NOT closely related to any other bird family; they make up their own order, known as Psittaciformes. It is the nature of taxonomy that the number and classification of species is always in flux. It's not easy to determine if a group of animals is a true species (meaning that it doesn't interbreed with other species). Evolution is ongoing. Some species are in transition, and data on interbreeding is often hard to gather. The classification system today splits the twenty-one species of cockatoos and cockatiels into the family Cacatuidae, and lumps the remaining 332 species of parrots, parakeets, conures, macaws, and lories into family Psittacidae. (Some scientists split the fifty-two species of nectar-eating lories and lorikeets, with their specialized tongues for extracting nectar from flowers, out of Psittacidae into their own family, Loriidae.)

The recent finding of a fossil cockatoo from the early to middle Miocene, about 40 million years ago, in northwest Queensland, Australia, confirms that parrots are an ancient group, with Australia as a center of their evolution. The oldest parrot (Psittacidae) fossil found, Paleaopsittacus georgei, is also about 40 million years old. The bird lived in southern England and was about a third as long as Tiko.

Members of Tiko's genus, Amazona, are stocky birds with short tails and rounded wings, wonderfully adapted to flying through dense forests and feeding in trees. They are strong, able to hang in any position while feeding, and their thick, fleshy tongues and strong bills are further aids in getting to a wide range of fruits and nuts. Most Amazons are green, with touches of bright red, orange, or blue on their heads and wings. Tiko's species, the Red-lored Amazon, is one of twenty-six species of Amazona; they range from southern Mexico to Ecuador, with an isolated population in the Amazon. His scientific name is *Amazona autumnalis*. The illustrations of Red-lored Amazons in most books feature the Mexican variety, with its bright yellow cheek patch. Tiko belongs to the subspecies called *salvini*, which is found from Nicaragua through Costa Rica and into northern South America. Salvini, instead of yellow, has a brilliant green patch on the cheeks.

Tiko's name comes from Costa Rica, whose people refer to themselves as "ticos," after their custom of adding the affectionate diminutive *tico* to the end of words. It's a popular name for a parrot, to judge by the letters I have seen in bird magazines. Although "Tiko" appears to be a misspelling, I received him as "Tiko," and "Tiko" he remains. Few, so far, have viewed the error with alarm, and Tiko scarcely mentions it.

THE HISTORY OF parrot-human interaction is long. About 130,000 years ago, Homo sapiens emerged in central Africa. Early humans most often hunted in open grassland, but a few went into the forests. These venturesome early hominids would have encountered noisy flocks of African Grey Parrots, beautiful silver-gray birds with a splash of bright red in the tail. They would have observed the parrots' knack for mimicking the birds and mammals around them, and they would have been intrigued. I can easily imagine some child putting out food for the pretty, entertaining creatures and returning to watch them each day. It is likely that the first parrot was tamed in this way.

From this first contact onward, the survival of parrots has been linked to human beings. In many tropical countries today, colorful birds as pets are as common as dogs and cats are in the United States. This takes its toll on a finite parrot population, but export of the birds is a far more serious problem. In a recent five-year span, more than 4.2 million parrots were legally exported, and this comprises but a small fraction of the real number, given the thriving trade in smuggled birds. Amazons, African Greys, and budgies, which make the best pets, are particularly at risk of overexploitation.

Nearly 80 percent of New World parrots in the pet trade today are destined for the United States. About 150,000 are smuggled into the U.S. across the Mexican border each year, and this is just one route for the activity. In the early 1990s, the United States legally imported at least 250,000 parrots a year (the figure is from the Worldwide Fund for Nature), worth in excess of $300 million. About four fifths of these birds were taken from the wild.

Horrific methods are used to capture wild parrots. I've encountered them in tropical forests around the world. In 1969 I visited the rain forests of Suriname, a small country on the northeast coast of South America. I'd just begun work toward my doctorate; though fairly certain I would study gulls for my Ph.D. research, I was still intrigued by the possibility of studying parrots in the tropics, and had gone to Suriname during Christmas break as a sort of scouting trip. I walked along a riverbank with two colleagues, our eyes riveted on the canopy above, hoping to catch a glimpse of one of the forest's splendors, the magnificent Scarlet Macaw. This bird, one of the larger parrots, is distinguished by its brilliant scarlet head and body, the red accented by striking blue-and-yellow wings and a splash of blue at the base of its tail. We spotted several Yellow-headed Amazons swooping through the trees. It was on this journey, more than thirty years ago, that I fell in love with Amazons.

I saw what appeared to be a coil of rope in a distant branch and recognized it instantly as a parrot noose. We soon found several more. A parrot steps into the noose as it maneuvers toward fruit, and as it walks forward along the branch the slack is taken up and the bird can't go on. It begins to retrace its steps, and the noose tightens. The bird frantically pecks the rope, but to no avail. There are only a few trees fruiting in the forest at any one time in any given area, and they bear fruit for just a few days. This is what makes this hunting method possible. The fruit brings the parrots, and the hunters will often wait near the trees. We looked nervously around, but saw no one. Whoever these people were, they knew how to climb: the nooses were set much too high for the three of us to take down. Saddened, we went on our way. It was a long time ago, but the thought of those nooses still causes a chill to go through me.

Not only are eggs, chicks, and adults removed from the wild to satisfy the pet trade, but nest trees are often destroyed in the process. Since the number of available nest holes is limited, this is a devastating loss for many a parrot population. Again, I've had firsthand experience with this approach to capturing parrots.

In March 1973, I visited the Peruvian rain forest on the way back from fieldwork in Argentina. I was still considering the possibility of doing work in the tropics. A friend and I were exploring a potential research site on the eastern slope of the Andes, below Machu Picchu, when we ran into a man walking through the forest. I wanted to see a Blue-headed Parrot, a chunky green bird with a delicate blue head, a black wash behind the eye, a yellow splash on the bend of its wing, and the red vent (underside) that gives it its species name, menstrus. I asked the stranger where we might find such a bird. He'd seen a pair the day before, and was happy to share his knowledge. It turned out, however, that he captured young parrots for a living. Because it was difficult to access their nest holes, he said, he cut down the trees in which they nested.

The thought made me ill. Here he was, felling one-hundred-year-old trees in order to capture three or four baby birds; after they had crashed to the ground and been separated from their parents, maybe one would live. But I tried not to judge him. Tropical hunters can make more money by delivering a healthy parrot than they would earn in a year by working the land, their traditional means of livelihood.

I kept asking him questions. The odd thing was that he loved parrots, and kept one as a pet. He respected them. His knowledge of their behavior and habitat was impressive. The hardest part of his job, he confided, was determining the best time to fell the tree: he had to capture the baby birds before they fledged and could fly away, yet if he brought the tree down too early the creatures would not be able to survive without their parents. His window of opportunity was narrow, perhaps two weeks.

This bizarre encounter in Peru took place before the worldwide conservation effort began. Hunters and poachers today are more furtive. It would be difficult at the beginning of the twenty-first century to find someone hunting parrots openly, and harder still to induce them to speak about their work.

TIKO, OF COURSE, was a captive-bred bird, so I didn't have to worry that he'd been yanked from his jungle home as a chick. The fact that he was captive-raised made it in a strange way especially thrilling to me when he took a giant step toward asserting his wild nature, his sense of independence, freedom, and mobility.

I was riding my exercise bike one evening while Mike was in the kitchen preparing dinner. Tiko had declined the invitation to join me, and he was upstairs, lording over the office. I had ceased, by that point, to insist on his company.

"Honey," Mike called, "baked or mashed?"

"Baked," I said. Seconds later in my peripheral vision I registered a stunning sight—Tiko banked hard into a swooping turn, sweeping effortlessly through the open door into the room. He maneuvered around the corner with precision, taking full advantage of the short round wings of his genus, which were meant for just this sort of cornering. He circumnavigated the room with vigorous shallow wingbeats, and landed on the bookshelf facing me, looking proud. He made a soft, delicate cooing sound.

I had stopped pedaling. Tiko had taken a spin around the kitchen on his historic flight down from the office, and Mike, jolted from his preparations, came barreling into the exercise room in Tiko's wake.

"Tiko, you genius! That was wonderful!" My heart soared. It was like watching a child take its first few steps. Better: it was like watching an animal regain its freedom.

His flights over the next few weeks were a constant source of joy, not just for me but for him. I loved seeing him career around the house, avoiding objects, turning corners, just as he would have done in Costa Rica's tropical lowlands. His navigational skills improved daily until he could make successive right-angle turns. He'd zip from room to room, sail gracefully down the stairs, and land on one of the library's topmost shelves. Perhaps the greatest thrill was to call him to me and watch him do a few turns around the house and then land unerringly on my shoulder.

When spring arrived I knew that Tiko, given his rediscovered expertise, would have liked to try the great outdoors. When parrots are raised in a backyard, as they often are in the tropics, they usually remain on the premises, at least in the area, even though free-flying. But Tiko was not in this category. The risk was not that he would "fly away," but that he might get lost. Mike and I now and then see free-flying parrots in the streets, usually forlorn, no longer anyone's pet. I did not want Tiko to become like them, or suffer the fate of Moomoo, Mike's cowbird, whose disappearance had brought us so much pain.

Some owners clip their parrot's flight feathers every time the bird molts. A bird so treated can still climb and glide, but cannot take flight. Clipping the wing feathers will also prevent indoor accidents—crashing into windows, breaking mirrors, knocking over vases or lamps, landing in the frying pan, or even falling into a toilet bowl, as once befell Tiko, who has not gone near one since. But we did not consider clipping: I wanted Tiko to remain as wild as a captive parrot with a New Jersey zip code can be.

I was especially wary because some years ago two local friends of ours, Paula and Ron Barfield, went to New England for a weekend to view the fall foliage. They took along their African Grey, named Alex, who traveled with them everywhere. Al was not much more than six months old, and he was adorable. He was learning to talk, and could say "Paula," much to her delight. The three were having breakfast on the patio of their hotel, enjoying the autumn sunshine. The bird saw a butterfly and started to chase it. He had never flown before, and the minute he lifted off he was blown by a gust of wind into the upper branches of a nearby tree. Unable to descend, he dangled upside down from a branch, squawking, "Hello, darling!" They had no way to reach the bird. A second gust pried the hapless parrot from the branch, blew him into the sky, over the woods, and out of sight. Ron and Paula remained at the hotel for days, combing the woods. To no avail—they never saw Alex again.

So we kept Tiko in the house. We diligently created an indoor environment that would stimulate him, one in which he would thrive. His ability to fly lessened his aggression and hostility somewhat, but still I often found him ornery and distant. Mike and I worked hard to close the gaps remaining between us and the bird—to better understand him. On many days, it seemed to us this would consume a lifetime. And I often wondered if we would ever achieve the closeness I so avidly desired.

4

The Parrots in My Past

THAT FIRST WINTER, AS MIKE AND I STRUGGLED TO ES-
tablish a harmonious household with our new addition, I would wonder if we had come into Tiko's life too late. Perhaps his bond with
Libby and Freda had simply been too strong, and the degree of intimacy he was either willing or able to establish with another human
being would always be qualified. I wondered, too, about my own
needs. Tiko was endlessly fascinating and often affectionate. Why did
I want more? On long dark winter evenings I was surprised to find
myself brooding about the relationship, a useless activity with which
I am generally impatient.

I'd had no time to brood growing up on the farm. Our life was all
about doing, or thinking about doing—and I like to think my science
has always benefited from my farm-girl upbringing. We had to think
about a wide range of different crops and the activities surrounding

their planting, cultivation, and harvest. Farming necessitated doing a number of different things at once, and keeping lots of projects on track simultaneously. We needed to be able to improvise constantly, depending on the weather and shifts in the market. We also had to keep our final goal in mind at all times.

I carried that over into the way I do science. People are often amazed at how much I do at once, but I guess I think of all scientific activities as if they were part of the vegetable and flower farm of my youth, which was diverse, complicated, and always iterative, always changing. We learned from our experience and tried new things, which is perhaps the main reason that my father is out there farming away at ninety. He works twelve-hour days. He keeps several balls in the air at once, juggling, never sitting still, always engaged, always thinking, planning, plotting, and loving every minute of it. It keeps him young, and I have tried to follow in his footsteps.

So that first winter I was upset to find myself staring into space in a kind of reverie, pondering my lifelong passion for birds and comparing my relationship to Tiko with the parrots in my past. You see, when Tiko came to me I was not a parrot neophyte. Parrots had preceded him in my heart. I secretly measured him against them, and, I am loath to admit, found him wanting.

One moment, it seemed, I was a girl dashing after Spotted Sandpiper chicks on my parents' farm, and the next I was in college, studying ornithology. I wasn't raised to be a scientist. In high school I had languished on the "secretarial track"; it was the benighted fifties, after all. It was assumed that I would find a husband after graduation, marking time meanwhile as a secretary, should Prince Charming be slow to appear. But in my junior year of high school I thought it might be fun to take a biology class. My guidance counselor made a valiant effort to dissuade me: "Those are college-bound kids in there! You'll never keep up!" My stubbornness surprised him, and in the end he relented.

I loved the class, did well in it, and Miss Richards, a teacher whose name I have reason to remember, persuaded the school principal that I was "college material" myself. They scrambled and got me into the State University of New York at Albany, to my family's surprise, if not delight.

There was an area of study known as field ornithology at Albany; hardly believing my luck, I was allowed my first semester to take a class in it. I lived at home and commuted to college. I didn't really belong to the bustling life on the campus, and yet I felt separate from my family, unable to participate as I had in the past in life on the farm. This state of limbo and its concomitant loneliness moved me to acquire a companion. In an Albany pet shop I found a bright blue Budgerigar—a small parakeet, native to Australia—that I named Lucinda after a mule in a book I had loved as a child.

Lucinda, my very first parrot, was a beautiful bird. She was diminutive, fitting easily in the palm of my hand. Her lustrous wing feathers were steel blue. She had a touch of bright canary yellow on her head and throat. Budgies are generally friendly, and Lucinda was no exception. I'd come home after classes and Lucinda would chirp excitedly, leaping in her cage. Her contact call, used to reestablish a relationship with a bird that's been away, was a pleasing warble, although she emitted a piercing two-note screech when summoning me from another room. She perched upon my hand and rode around the house on my shoulder. Her notion of being affectionate was a gentle nip on the finger or ear, which didn't do much damage. She became distraught if I was home and left her in her cage, although my parents said she seemed content enough to occupy it when I was away. During my absence the cage was her refuge; she spent hours swinging from her perch and chewing up the small willow or apple branches I had put in for her entertainment. She never did learn to talk, although she was gifted at mimicking other birds. Bent over my books, I'd all at once hear the "Caw! Caw! Caw!" of a crow, the "Thunk! Thunk!" of a Pileated Woodpecker working on a tree, or a Bluejay's strident call. And there would be Lucinda, her tiny chest thrust forward, her beak pointed to the ceiling, belting out her imitations with verve and humor. She might be responding to an actual call, or (just for the fun of it) dredging one from memory, but I date my love affair with parrots to those moments.

ONLY AFTER I HAD graduated with a degree in biology was my family persuaded to raise its sights for me. Off I went to Cornell for a master's degree in zoology and science education. Lucinda died just as I was leaving for Cornell. I mourned her passing but never doubted that I would one day replace her with another parrot. I was smitten by them, and I knew it.

I landed a teaching job at the State University of New York (SUNY) College at Buffalo, and then, at twenty-eight, entered the doctorate program in animal behavior at the University of Minnesota.

Minnesota seemed exotic, distant. Boston, until then, was the farthest I'd ever been from home. My doctorate thesis was on Franklin's Gull, a small bird with a black head and bright-red bill and feet. In the late 1960s, little was known about them, and thousands of pairs nested within a four-hour drive of the university, in the cattail marshes of northwest Minnesota.

I was about a year and a half into my research when Sam, a Red-lored Amazon, like Tiko, came into my life. It was a rich time for me: gulls by day, a parrot at night. Unlike Tiko, who was hatched in captivity, Sam had arrived in the country in the company of Walt Graul, a friend of mine from graduate school. Walt had bought him as a fledgling in Mexico, and they had lived together for four years, becoming very close. When Walt married, however, the parrot objected to the bride's presence in the bedroom, and expressed his dissatisfaction by flying directly at her face. After a few such assaults Sam was banished to his cage, permitted to exit only when Walt's wife was away. The problem worsened once the couple had a child: Sam took umbrage at the affection Walt lavished on his daughter. When she was three, the little girl somehow persuaded her mother to let Sam out of his cage, with predictable results. When the bird tried to savage both females, Walt received an ultimatum from his wife: the parrot or us. My old friend carefully weighed the matter, but in the end Sam lost out and was offered to me.

I set about making friends with the pugnacious Amazon. He had not had much experience with a cordial female voice, and was taken with it when he heard it. It helped, of course, that I let him fly around the apartment for most of the day—he loved being out of his cage.

Unlike Tiko, the transference of his affections to me was instant and complete. When Walt came to visit several weeks later he was greeted with a raucous call that clearly meant "Stay away." The sight of Walt conveyed to Sam the threat of renewed confinement in a cage. It was a tough moment for Walt, but he was adult about it; through the sharp pangs of rejection he managed to rejoice at Sam's good fortune.

SAM AND I MOVED to a postdoctoral position at Rutgers' Institute of Animal Behavior, where I was to do further research on marsh-nesting gulls, this time Brown-hooded Gulls, which nest in the pampas marshes of Argentina. Of course, there was the question of Sam. I didn't let on, as we drove from Minneapolis to Newark, New Jersey, that our move to Rutgers would probably result in a separation. The bird loved being on the road, and sat contentedly in his cage as the states rolled by. When it was cool enough, I rolled up the windows and opened his cage. He would perch on the back of my seat and sound off, sometimes so loudly that passengers in passing cars heard him even with the windows closed. He scared the living daylights out of several people. When he was bored he would nibble on the collar of my shirt or preen my hair.

Since I was going to be at the institute for only a few weeks be-fore traveling to Argentina, it seemed foolish to look for an apart-ment. Besides, I had heard that Newark was not the safest place for a single woman. So Sam and I moved into my office at the institute. I felt secure; Smith Hall was a fortress.

During the day Sam remained sedately in his cage, keeping an eye on the parade of people moving through the office, or else catching up on sleep. But at night I opened the door to his cage and he flew through the hallways, banking smartly around the corners like a feathered Ferrari. He sometimes had to swerve wildly to dodge the unsuspecting coming the other way. Usually he was agile enough to avoid them, and in any event, no one was ever hurt. Nor was I worried about him getting lost—he seemed to add to his excursions just a little every day, as if sketching the floor plan of the building in his head.

I loved those evening hours. Few people were about, it was peaceful, and I got much more work done than I did during the day. The campus police who patrolled the halls came to know my routine. Living in an office was certainly unusual, if not illegal, but the police simply added me to their rounds. If I became hungry during the night they would escort me through the tough Newark streets to a local restaurant for a roast beef sandwich, which was probably a pleasant break from their usual routine. They took to bringing Sam goodies, and in this way we discovered his sweet tooth. The bird and I would join the police during their breaks in the seminar room, and Sam would pop around sipping from our sodas. He appeared to have a preference for Coke, but made sure to drink from every cup, as if asserting his dominance.

By late September he had grown fond of several of my colleagues at the institute, so when I went to Argentina I was comfortable leaving him behind. Rae Silver, doing her Ph.D. on Ring Doves, would open my office door each morning, chat with Sam, and give him fresh water and food, usually seeds, peanuts, fruits, and vegetables. While he didn't talk, Sam would respond to Rae with a series of intricate calls. In the evening, the security police would often let him fly around the halls, returning him to his cage when they were finished with their rounds. I left for Argentina confident that Sam was in good hands.

AGAINST ALL ADVICE, I went to South America without knowing Spanish. Only my Ph.D. adviser, H. B. Tordoff, did not try to talk me out of it. He knew how stubborn I was. "You're going to go anyway, so I might as well help you," he said, and introduced me to Milt Weller and several other ornithologists who had worked in Argentina. Milt put me in touch with Peter Miles, who was himself very interested in birds, and who helped me find a place to study the gulls near his *estancia* (cattle ranch). Peter's forefathers came to Argentina from Britain in the 1800s. He and other descendants of these original colonists now owned many of the region's large ranches, thought of themselves as British, and spoke English.

I lived in Sante Fe Province, near Venado Tuerto, in an abandoned gaucho mud hut with no door or windows, and only Plains Vizcachas, large grayish-brown rodents, and black snakes for company. An old barbed-wire fence kept the cows from coming into the hut and provided me with a small pasture where I could hang my clothes to dry; it also gave the Burrowing Owls a place to nest where they would not be trampled by livestock. The closest English speakers, Peter and his family, lived fifty miles away; my nearest neighbors were the gauchos who tended the cattle herds of their wealthy landowner. The gauchos quickly accepted me as part of their family, although they scratched their heads in wonder at the gringo men who allowed a female family member to be so far from home alone. The gaucho matriarch, Madre, felt obliged to adopt me; she chaperoned me everywhere. Everywhere, that is, except to the gull colony in the marsh.

Gato, one of Madre's sons, a handsome bachelor about my own age, was especially protective. He lent me a horse, and often rode with me to check on the nests in the gull colony. The gauchos spent long hours riding the open grassland of the pampas, and Gato knew the secret nest locations of several of the birds I was eager to observe: grebes, herons, and Painted Snipes. Many of the pampas herons and egrets were the same species that we're familiar with up north, but the grebes were different. The metallic-gray Silvery Grebe, handsome and secretive, particularly intrigued me.

I eventually told my adopted family about Sam, and how much I missed him. Not long afterward, Gato appeared at my hut with a recently fledged Nanday Conure, a small green parrot with a black face and a tinge of blue on her chest. I was happy to have her and touched by the gesture. I named her Sue.

My Spanish at the time was still not deep enough for me to be certain how Gato had acquired the bird. But I was being tutored by Laura, one of Gato's sisters, and in time was given to understand that the bird had come from the Chaco area, in northern Sante Fe Province, and that Gato had traveled there by bus to get her from a friend, who had rescued her from a recent blowdown. The fallen tree, Laura said, was miles from the nearest dirt road, but the gauchos, who spent long days riding the pampas looking for injured cows or broken fences, knew the whereabouts of all manner of creatures, and once Gato spread the word that he needed a young conure, it took no more than a week for the vast gaucho network to find one.

My own way of communicating across the fifty miles separating me from my English host was via carrier pigeon. It would be a better way for me to reach him, Peter said, than the antiquated phone system, which in any case I had no access to. Every other week I'd attach my grocery list to a pigeon's leg and toss it in the air, wishing it godspeed on its fifty-mile journey. A couple of days later Peter would show up in his Jeep, with my groceries, mail, and a fresh pigeon.

SUE WAS A LOVELY SHADE of bright green, her black face and blue chest setting off her red thighs and yellowish breast and belly. Her tail was long and pointed. From the tip of her bill to the tip of her tail she was only about twelve inches long, a soft, cuddly creature. For the first day or two she slept in a small cardboard box next to my cot, nestled in a bed of my soft cotton shirts. She slept on her back with her feet in the air; when I saw her this way for the first time I was sure she was dead. I called out to her and rushed to pick her up. She responded with a loud squawk and a flashing of her eyes, clear signs of her displeasure at having been so rudely awakened.

In a few days she had developed enough strength in her legs to sit at the edge of the overturned milk crate I used as a nightstand, and she no longer slept on her back. She tucked her bill in her back feathers and slept just inches from my head. When the early morning light seeped into the hut, she'd step off the milk crate, climb into my sleeping bag, and snuggle down next to my chest. I'd wake to her soft squeals as she settled in. She was incredibly loving and affectionate, unlike older parrots, who have developed a sense of independence. I was not alone in finding her irresistible. Both Laura and Gato took to bringing her treats when they came to visit, and she would sometimes cheerfully alight on their shoulders in thanks. The soft homemade flat bread Laura brought was her particular favorite.

Perched on my shoulder, Sue accompanied me everywhere except the marsh. She loved the long trips we made to neighbors, riding on my shoulder as I galloped across the pampas. She would cling to me tightly, leaving tiny claw marks. She loved the wheat-flour noodles Madre and her daughters made (and taught me to make), which they put into a stew. Like most young parrots, she adapted well to new people, eagerly climbing from one shoulder to another. In a few weeks she'd picked up several words, and used them constantly whenever anyone was there to hear. "Hello!" she'd scream, or *"Pase!"* (Come in!) to whomever appeared at the door. She loved the way Madre yelled, "Joanna!" and mimicked her tone so precisely that I was misled several times. Her vocabulary was limited—she'd found a few words that pleased her, and they seemed to suffice. I never tired of hearing her call, "Joanna!" at the top of her tiny lungs. It was a wonderful homecoming, as I waded across the open water of the marsh at the end of the day, toward the hut and the setting sun. She learned to fly above me as I galloped across the pampas, raucously screeching, "Kree-ah!"—an exact expression of my own joyous sense of freedom as I covered miles of open space under enormous skies.

Even with all the support I had from the gauchos and Peter, I think I would have found my time in the pampas almost unbearably lonely if not for Sue. We became very close, and I learned from her invaluable lessons about the true nature of companionship, which can extend across species' lines. The comfort, joy, and enlivening sense we shared in each other's presence felt like a gift to me. There was something of the miraculous in it. So it was with a sense of heartache that finally, five months after my arrival, it came time to leave—and I decided, after agonizing about it, to leave Sue behind. It would have been extremely hard for her to make the trip to the United States. This was the time of the Newcastle disease panic, and importing a parrot was nearly impossible. I would have had to get an import permit, and then subject her to weeks of quarantine by U.S. Customs. The object of the quarantine, of course, is to keep poultry disease from entering the country, not to keep incoming birds healthy. Many die of loneliness and starvation, and I could not bear to subject Sue to the process.

I left her with Gato. They were quite fond of each other, and I knew he'd take good care of her. For months after my return to the institute, I received letters from Gato telling me how much Sue missed me, how she called out my name every day. She would fly away from him and he'd find her sitting forlornly in my abandoned hut, perched on the milk crate, beside the empty cot. She would go with him when he came for her, but the next day she'd leave again, flying miles across the pampas to my hut, calling, "Joanna! Joanna!" over the rolling grasslands.

ONE PARROT'S LOSS was another's gain. Sam was delighted to have me back, though he'd been well seen to by Rae, who reported that he had eaten, exercised, and socialized daily. But I admit I was happy to see that no one had edged aside the leading lady in his life. When I first returned he refused to leave my side, staying as close to me as he could, preening my fingers and toes for hours at a time. We settled into our old routine at the institute, the bird babbling nonstop and tucking his head under my fingers, interrupting my work, waiting for me to scratch his nape. His schedule didn't vary; he hung out in the office all day while I worked, and flew around the empty halls at night. Where I went, he went.

Only a few weeks after my return, I left again, this time with Sam, to do turtle research on Little Beach Island on the Jersey Shore, near Brigantine. The university research station was a lovely old Coast Guard post, since burned down. Sam quickly endeared himself to my fellow researchers, who brought him treats. He was willing enough to accept the goodies, but took a dim view of people who entered my room while I was gone. If you popped in during my absence with a treat for him he'd take it, then strenuously invite you to depart. He didn't often bite—a sharp squawk and lunge usually did the trick.

Some mornings I'd go down to the beach before dawn to look for female turtles plodding along the sand in search of nest sites. It was important to be out there at high tide, when the turtles would leave the water. The distance to the high dunes, where they would nest, was shortest then. I left while it was still dark, and picked my way down to the beach to wait for dawn. When I spotted a female hunting for a site, I'd creep stealthily along the dunes, keeping far enough back so that the vibrations of my footsteps didn't spook her.

Sam never grew accustomed to my predawn excursions. If he awoke and found me gone he called out for half an hour, a raucous, unabated screeching I could hear a mile away. I shuddered, knowing he was summoning me back the way a wild parrot frantically yells for its mate, or any member of its flock, should it wake to find itself alone. "Where is everybody?" The call was very different from the one Tiko gave at Josie's; that mournful screech did not stop when she entered the room. But I fear such distinctions were lost on my housemates, who were still asleep when Sam's alarm went off.

Eventually, I put dark shades on all the windows, which hoodwinked him into thinking it was still night. When I tiptoed out to look for turtles, he remained asleep. Upon my return I would open the shades, and he'd wake up to find me there. He was happy, and the rest could sleep a little longer.

My fellowship at the institute was for a year; I had no clear idea what I would be doing in the fall. Academic jobs for scientists were scarce. Nixon had slashed the funding available from the National Institutes of Health and the National Science Foundation for aspiring postdoctoral academics. A large number of highly qualified Ph.D.s were suddenly unemployed, and seeking academic posts. Worse, there were few women in the sciences—discrimination against women was taken as a matter of course (Madame Curie notwithstanding, science was supposed to be a man's domain)—and I was, frankly, apprehensive about my prospects.

WHEN THE NEW BRUNSWICK campus of Rutgers embarked on a national search for an expert in animal behavior, they called the institute for suggestions. I was reasonably certain that my chances were nil. Luckily my postdoc adviser, Colin Beer, who was utterly baffled by gender discrimination, described me to the department as "the best person in the country for fieldwork in animal behavior." I felt slightly sheepish about such a laudatory recommendation, but it seemed to do the trick. The rest of the old-boy network went along with Colin, and I got the job.

Sam and I went to the New Brunswick campus that fall, and I became an assistant professor in biology. Sam once again set up shop in my office. I was not living there, exactly, but it was where I spent almost all my time, including weekends. The life of an assistant professor was no day at the beach. I had to develop and teach several courses, apply for (and get) grants, and do research leading to scientific publication. In those days there were no start-up funds for field or laboratory equipment, no time off from teaching to set up a lab or work on grant applications, no assistants to help with the cumbersome undergraduate labs in ecology. It's hard to fathom now how things were structured back then. Today, a newly appointed assistant professor in biology is excused entirely from teaching duties for the first year or two. But I was teaching three classes each semester, working individually with graduate students, applying for grants, writing and publishing. It was the only way to advance. An assistant professor has to prove herself within the first five years; if she doesn't, she's out of a job. I was stretched to the limit. But I loved the challenge of it. I had finally found my place in the world and was doing exactly what I wanted to do.

At the same time I worried. The old-boy network would not slumber forever. Also, Rutgers required a minimum of three letters from well-known professors at other universities who were familiar with your work, and there were no women in positions to make such an evaluation. I had no doubt that my first name alone would put off some of the males. Nevertheless, I was often so blissfully lost in work that I forgot about the long-term prospects for my career.

It was also a rich time in my personal life, during which I developed a diverse and interesting circle of friends. I had been married once for six months in graduate school, an experiment that failed, in large part, because of the conflicting demands of two Ph.D.s in ornithology looking for the same jobs at the same time. He found a position in Washington, D.C., and I was faced with the choice of tagging along with him or chasing my own career. Thanks to the resilience of youth and the brevity of the marriage, I emerged unscathed. My stay in Argentina had been filled with adventure, and for now I enjoyed being single and hard at work. And, of course, there was Sam.

In those days, Sam was my main man. He perched beside my desk, watching my every move. He more or less ignored the rest of the world except for one colleague, whom he seemed to despise. I was amused by this; I liked the guy. But Sam became hostile whenever he appeared. He would pace on his perch, wings held slightly away from his body, head lowered and feathers fluffed. A bird will hold its wings that way only on the verge of flight, to avoid predators or to go on the attack. He did not relax until this colleague departed.

How did Sam know this guy was bad news? His keen hearing might have picked up revealing inflections in his tone, or perhaps Sam was responding to aggressive mannerisms that eluded me. He was clearly giving me a warning, but I paid it no heed. Then, one evening while I was working late, the man barged into my office, grabbed me around the waist, and forcibly kissed me. Out of the corner of my eye I saw Sam race back and forth at the edge of the desk, beak poised, wings outstretched. I screamed, Sam screeched, but there was no one to hear us. I was being pushed back over the desk when Sam flew to my shoulder and landed several savage pecks on the man's cheek and temple. He shielded his face, cried out, backed off. Sam went after him, screeching and beating his wings. While all this was going on I managed to edge my assailant out the door and lock it behind him.

I was trembling. I could barely stand. Sam returned to my shoulder and just sat there, still as stone. Then I felt him quiver. I remained in the office for I don't know how long, unable to move. The building was deserted, but I thought I heard footsteps in the hall. As I listened at the door, I thought I heard sounds at the window. Afraid that my assailant might break the glass, I called the campus police and asked them to walk me to my car. I told them what had happened, but didn't name the man. Sexual harassment (to dignify it so) in the mid-1970s was not all that rare, and there was little recourse when it happened.

I also feared that pointing a finger at a senior colleague would scuttle my chances of ever getting tenure.

The attacker returned the following day to shamefacedly apologize, but Sam was in no rush to forgive or forget. For years afterward he would pace frantically whenever this guy appeared. Once, without provocation, over a year after the incident, Sam shot off his perch and pecked furiously at the culprit's face and hands. Other colleagues, animal behaviorists themselves, were baffled by Sam's animosity, which I also professed not to understand.

EVERYONE BROUGHT SAM TREATS of one sort or another. Even when I wasn't there, friends and colleagues stopped by to say hello to him. He became fond of Bert Murray and Charlie Leck, both of whom did research in the behavior and ecology of birds. They were around often, usually armed with peanuts and grapes, pretzels and carrot sticks. Toward the end of the day, when the building was student-free, Sam would zoom through the halls, making U-turns and pirouettes on the way back to my office.

If I was late arriving in the morning, Sam would start to squawk. People soon learned that if they opened the door to my office he would assume I was around and quiet down. It also helped if they fed him. He was spoiled rotten. Colleagues soon felt confident enough to let him out of his cage, even with the office door open. He would sit on the cage-top and observe the students moving to and fro. But if I failed to arrive by late afternoon, he would deem it time to make a statement, and this he did by systematically shredding any book that might have been left open on my desk. He'd cut the pages into neat, one-inch strips and scatter them around the room. Sometimes, if deeply irritated by my absence, he'd clamber about my shelves and bite pieces out of books. He once ate some pages of my thesis, which I like to think was not an editorial comment. He was strong enough to pull slim volumes from the shelves. I'd get back from a weekend at the farm, where I'd been visiting my parents, and it was like a ticker-tape parade had passed through the room. I was annoyed, amused, and felt guilty all at once. Sam behaved this way only when I left him alone too long.

Sam caught cold each winter, and I worried about his health. I knew a great deal about the vulnerability of birds, and whenever I used solvents to clean my instruments, or painted my bird models, I locked Sam in another office. He was not happy with the arrangement, but I had no choice. Fumes will kill a parrot, or any bird, in a matter of minutes, sometimes seconds. Once you notice them gasping for breath, you've waited too long. Their susceptibility to respiratory problems is what causes a bimodal life span for parrots in captivity; they either die fairly young from pulmonary distress or, somehow immune to such problems, live into old age. People can spend hundreds of dollars on a spectacular bird, shower it with affection, and lose it within a few years.

Unlike mammals, which can be sick for weeks before recovering or dying, birds are not very likely to recover from illness, and tend to go very quickly. They have an extensive system of air sacs in their abdominal cavity and bones, which makes their bodies light and helps them fly but also makes them susceptible to airborne diseases and fumes. Birds can die from the fumes of household cleaners, the propellant from aerosols (such as hair spray and cleaners, spray starch, and nonstick sprays used to coat cooking utensils), paint fumes, and natural gas leaks. Even the polytetrafluoroethylene gas released from nonstick pots left too long on a stove is dangerous—if heated above 530 degrees Fahrenheit, the fumes are deadly. This is why canaries were taken down into coal mines, as recently as the 1950s in the United States. If there were any toxic gases present, the canary stopped singing and soon died, in time for the miners to exit before they too were affected.

As careful as I was to keep Sam from deadly pathogens, I couldn't prevent his winter colds. They were chronic, and one bitter day, when he was sniffing and sneezing, his condition suddenly worsened. The sneezing—little high-pitched huffs with a spasm in his chest and a ruffling of feathers, followed by a baleful glance—intensified, and he began to cough. I couldn't coax him from his cage. He stopped eating and sat hunched with his feathers fluffed. Days passed and still he barely ate. He was clearly growing weaker.

I called around and found a vet who was said to be knowledgeable about birds. A colleague rushed Sam and me to his office. I was too shaken to drive, and I wanted to hold my parrot in my lap. The vet injected an antibiotic, but he must have misgauged Sam's size and weight, for on the way back to Rutgers my poor parrot's condition worsened dramatically, as though he had received an overdose. I sat in my office, holding him in my hands. Friends got the news and trickled in, for Sam was dear to many.

I felt the life draining from him. He cuddled into my palms, his breath shallow and quick. His eyes slowly closed and then he grew still and his breath stopped. I wept as my friend Ron (whose own baby parrot, years later, would be carried off by a gust of wind) took him from me and wrapped him in a towel.

Ron made the funeral arrangements—I was too upset to do so. Later that day, nearly forty people gathered beneath my window, where we buried Sam. The service was multidenominational. I wrapped him in a piece of treasured embroidery from Argentina and gently placed him in the earth.

He had been with me while I labored to finish my Ph.D., during my heady postdoctoral days, when I got my first job, and while I taught my first classes. He had defended me from an attacker. He had been unstinting in his willingness to offer me comfort and affection. For almost six years he had been my constant companion. His loss was a terrible blow, and I miss him still.

So it was in those early difficult days with Tiko I often thought of my Sam. How could Tiko possibly measure up? And how would I, in Tiko's life, ever be able to replace Freda and Libby? Tiko and I forged some ties, but as yet—and perhaps it was unreasonable to hope for this—there was nothing like the closeness I had had with Sam, or with Sue, for that matter. I think I'd even felt closer to my little Lucinda. As I sat at my desk in protective eyeglasses and a long-sleeved shirt, I often found myself idly caressing my talisman, a single feather (green and red) that had once adorned the body of my loyal friend and fearless protector, Sam.

5

Our Morning Ritual

WHEN HE HAD BEEN WITH US FOR ABOUT FIVE MONTHS, Tiko began molting. One day I found two small green feathers on the floor of the office. By the following week virtually every surface in the house was littered with shimmering green. Parrots, like most birds, have several thousand feathers (waterbirds have thirteen to fifteen thousand, an adaptation to life on the water), which are usually molted gradually. Tiko's molt was really quite sudden, as if he hadn't shed a feather until he was sure he could trust us.

After he had shed his body feathers for about three weeks, his wing feathers began to fall, both the "primaries"—the ten feathers attached to the ends of the wings—and the secondary feathers, which begin where the primaries end and continue up to where the wings join the body.

Delicate structures that they are, feathers must be regularly replaced. After a migrating bird has traveled a great distance, the ends of its flight feathers have been partly worn away by wind resistance and contact with the ground or vegetation, just as a flag frays. Even for stay-at-homes like Tiko, daily flight and climbing around the house results in considerable wear and tear.

Birds molt about twice a year; new feathers push out the old, much as adult teeth push out baby ones. Birds in flocks tend to molt simultaneously, and birds never molt during the breeding season, when their energy must be conserved for the task at hand. Most migratory birds change their feathers between the breeding season and their journey.

All parrots molt the same way, beginning in the middle of the wing, with one or two primary feathers. This allows the bird to continue to fly during the molt. There are exceptions: most ducks will lose a number of their wing feathers all at once, so that for a short period during their molt they're grounded. But ducks have the advantage of being able to live on water, where they are protected from most predators and can feed efficiently even when they're unable to fly. Molting parrots in the wild generally remain in the tops of fruiting trees, relying on their climbing abilities to forage and stay out of harm's way. They seldom fly from one branch to another while foraging in any case, usually climbing around the tree with their claws and beak as though they were on a giant jungle gym.

Tiko's wing tips are black, an evolutionary adaptation that makes them stronger. The dark pigment in feathers offers resistance to wear and abrasion, and is fairly common in birds. But the many miles an Amazon must fly daily to get from its roost to its food supply, even with its black-tipped wings, leaves its feathers worn by molting time.

Tiko should have molted his primary and secondary feathers symmetrically, losing a feather from one side and then, within a day or two, losing the same feather on the other. But his molt was haphazard. More feathers fell out than should have, and more from one side than the other, which made it difficult for him to fly. This embarrassed him considerably. His molt lasted just under two months, and his new feathers were resplendent. The pale orange became an orange-red, then dull red, then vibrant red, as the feathers grew in. The blue tint on his head reappeared and, gradually, subtle shades of green replaced his dull olive hue.

As I watched Tiko's color return, I saw him being reborn. The transformation of his external self seemed to signal a sea change in his internal world as well. With the molt he shed much of his suspicion: he was truly a bird of a different feather. This, of course, also had to do with my own frame of mind; the molt and the brilliance of his fresh feathers renewed my sense of confidence in my role as a caretaker in Tiko's life. His—or, rather, our—mutual adoption had not been a mistake; he was thriving. And as his new feathers came in, he finally bonded with me.

The fateful act that signaled that Tiko and I had begun to travel down the long road to feverish rendezvous under the credenza came unexpectedly. It was a warm spring evening; sap was rising. An aroma of *amour,* as the French say, was in the air—an aroma to which my husband and I were not immune. It is not without irony that I remember feeling that sense of inseparability, the kind of ineffable closeness that comes in marriage when you feel blended into the thoughts and moods of your mate. I was snipping the first fresh herbs of the season, parsley and sage, from the potted plants by the open kitchen window. The evening light was soft and a warm breeze came in, bathing my neck and face, wafting through my hair. Mike moved in behind me and I smelled his smell and heard him say my name, softly, in almost a whisper, and I felt his hands on me and then . . . all hell broke loose!

Tiko emitted an ear-piercing squawk, sprang from his aerie atop the Frigidaire, and in one fell swoop was on my shoulder. He lunged at Mike, clearly trying to drive him away. I was puzzled, but only for a moment. A vision of Sam flashed through my mind as he drove away my attacker. Tiko had leaped to my defense! I was sure that at that very moment he had bonded with me. Mike caught my eye, smiled, and backed away. But Tiko did not stop squawking until my husband left the room. He had claimed me as his own.

WITH HIS BONDING, Tiko finally joined the family. He now had a clear position in our little world—mate to me, and alpha parrot of our flock. It all clicked for him. He stationed himself in a high place and gazed imperiously down on us and on the rest of his domain. He kept me company while I rode my exercise bike, or while I selected my clothes and jewelry in my dressing room; if Mike, forgetful, entered either place, he would soon be in full retreat, protecting his bare toes or ears.

Tiko no longer invited Mike to preen him. He flew only to my side, cooing softly, whenever the preening urge struck. He became extremely possessive of me, flashing his eyes at Mike and even buzzing him if he thought he detected any hint of amorous design. Luckily for Tiko, and for me, all this did not diminish Mike's keen interest in the bird's behavior, nor lessen the pleasure he took in the pleasure Tiko was clearly giving me. He was man enough not to feel threatened by a parrot—at least not yet! Mike was happy to be a member of our little flock, albeit hovering much of the time on the periphery of the inner circle, the exclusive pair bond.

The three of us developed a morning ritual, which continues to this day. Mike rolled out of bed hours before I stirred. He trudged upstairs, clicked on the light, and began working at his desk. At first Tiko would wake when Mike entered the office, but after a while he came to his senses—no self-respecting parrot chooses to face a world still in darkness. He slept instead for another hour or so, then called out, "Hello!" which was Mike's signal to open the cage door and carry him to his office perch. If Mike dawdled, Tiko uttered a single sharp squawk. If this too failed, he commenced the series of ear-shattering, raucous shrieks familiar to anyone who has lived with an Amazon, who sound each dawn as though they've been set on fire and are slowly burning.

Tiko expected me to be at his side as the day's business began. But I wasn't at my desk, I wasn't in the bathroom, I wasn't even in my dressing room. Where could I be? In time he realized that I was still in bed, and that if he fluttered onto the banister in the hall he could obtain a clear view of my sleeping form. The princely parrot was too discreet, too considerate, to wake me. But now he insisted that Mike, upon hearing his "Hello!" which broached no delay, shuttle him to the banister outside the bedroom, where his view of me was unobstructed. He was quiet and content, his eyes half closed, or his head turned into his downy, pistachio-colored back feathers, waiting patiently until I came to.

When I began to stir, usually around seven, his eyes flicked open and he glided into the bedroom and flapped up onto the bed. Then he began to slowly preen me, working his tongue over the tops of my fingers, probing gently and delicately with his bill and tongue, pulling off stray bits of skin and trimming my nails. I could hear his breathing, and a soft churring sound that came from deep within his throat. It was a lullaby meant just for me. I loved these moments, swimming up from sleep and becoming aware of what was happening. When he judged me able to respond he lowered his head, and I scratched the soft feathers at the back of his neck.

This mutual preening, known as allopreening, is an important part of life for mated parrots in the wild. They sit alongside each other for hours, alternately preening and sleeping. The preening is critical for maintaining feather health. If you've ever run your fingers through a feather, you know how the smooth surface on either side of the shaft (or calamus) is actually made up of a series of narrow filaments, called barbs. If you studied these barbs under a microscope you would find that they, in turn, are fringed with a series of still smaller filaments, or barbules, which have hooks that interlock with hooks on neighboring barbs. When Tiko preens, he pulls each feather through his bill, which rehooks its barbules, so that the feather forms a rigid unbroken surface. He waterproofs and lubricates this surface by picking up oil in his beak from a gland at the base of his tail. The tight surface provides an important form of protection against the elements, and an airfoil for flight. Body feathers are shorter, less stiff, and softer to the touch. These feathers, too, must be preened—preening keeps feathers clean and maintains their insulating properties. A bird also allopreens its mate's head and neck—spots where feathers would otherwise go untended.

Allopreening has a basic function beyond keeping hard-to-reach feathers healthy—it strengthens the bond between mated parrots, just as physical affection and sex do in human beings. Parrots' sexual relationships are limited to a short window each year, the week or two before and during egg-laying, when a pair will copulate dozens of times a day. But parrots remain physically connected, intimate through preening. Should a parrot quarrel with its mate, or for that matter with its human companion, allopreening can repair the relationship. I've witnessed a number of squabbles between mated parrots in the wild. Once, as I watched a pair feed together in a tree, one of the birds began to nibble on its mate's piece of fruit. The mate's short, aggressive call was followed by a lunge. The offending bird shied away, backing up along the branch. It took only seconds for the aggressor to have a change of heart. Forgetting the fruit, it sidled up to its spurned companion and tentatively preened its neck. On other occasions, I've seen one of a pair of allopreening parrots decide it no longer wants to be preened, and move angrily away. Sometimes it will drive its point home with a lunge. But after its mate backs away it will often change its tune, approach, and begin to preen the other bird.

It surprised me to learn that Tiko seemed intuitively to know the contours of my body. He worked diligently, one morning, to remove the bandage that covered a blister on my toe. As he cared for my body, I felt myself transported into a much more physically attentive kind of life than we're used to in this society. I was reminded of the Masai of Kenya, who spend hours dislodging prickers, thorns, and insects from their loved ones. I thought of a mother who every night, in a ritual full of meaning and pleasure for them both, brushes her daughter's hair. Tiko made me aware of how much richer our lives are when we have that kind of protracted ritualized form of physical contact, often accompanied, as it was with Tiko, by soft sounds, or in the case of human beings, by quiet intimate conversation carried along by the thread of a physical connection.

In fact, it was through his preening that Tiko inspired me to undertake a cross-species inquiry into grooming and preening, so as to explore what connections, if any, might exist between animal and human behavior in establishing intimacy. We naturally assume that such higher-level interactions are peculiar to humans, or perhaps to mammals. But the research I did indicated otherwise. It became clear to me that allopreening in birds had its corollaries in primate and, indeed, human behavior, and that in long-lived birds, such as parrots, it formed a central part of their existence.

Where parrots preen, primates groom (grooming refers to hair, preening to feathers). Parrots live in small flocks, but sometimes travel in flocks of one hundred members or more, and usually only mated pairs preen each other. All higher-order primates (monkeys, chimps, baboons, gorillas, and orangutans), on the other hand, selectively groom other members of their group, which helps them to maintain stable, long-term relationships between parents and young, males and females, and among siblings. Grooming keeps the group's relationships clear; it's all-important who can groom whom and when. All members of a small, tightly knit primate band are aware of who their relatives are and interact accordingly.

In Kenya, studying the grooming behavior of baboons, I noticed that when an adult groomed a baby, the adult doing the grooming also kept a lookout for danger. But when one adult baboon groomed another, the one being groomed kept the watch. Thus the animal doing the grooming entrusted the other with its life. How interesting, I thought, that the recompense for doing the grooming is the opportunity to become less aware of danger, to enter a kind of trance, which, in one sense, may be more relaxing and replenishing than being touched or touching another.

The lack of vigilance in the baboons that were doing the grooming intrigued me, and I returned to Kenya to research it further. There were complexities in grooming behavior that I saw had not been fully explored in scientific literature. I found myself chomping at the bit to become involved in the scientific debate around the subject.

My interest was twofold. First, a number of articles published in the early 1990s had suggested that an animal placed itself at greater risk of predation when it groomed another member of its group.* In

*D. Maestripieri, "Vigilance Costs of Allogrooming in Macaque Mothers," *American Naturalist*, vol. 141, 1993, pp. 744–53; L. A. Isbell and T. P. Young, "Social and Ecological Influences on Activity Budgets of Vervet Monkeys, and Their Implications for Group Living," *Behavioral Ecology and Sociobiology*, vol. 32, 1993, pp. 117–42; L. M. Rose and L. M. Fedigan, "Vigilance in White-Faced Capuchins, *Cebus capucinus*, in Costa Rica," *Animal Behavior*, vol. 49, 1995, pp. 63–70; Marina Cords, "Predator Vigilance Costs of Allogrooming in Wild Blue Monkeys," *Behaviour*, vol. 132, 1995, pp. 559–69.

evolutionary terms, this made little sense. Allogrooming is a common behavior in primates, and if it endangered individuals it seemed to me that it would have been eliminated long ago.

In the second place, the observation that an adult baboon entrusted its life to the individual it was grooming fascinated me. Animals in the wild tend to look out for themselves at all times. Here was a rare case in which a grown animal appeared to willingly place itself in a position of dependence on another. This fact, if indeed it was a fact, might upset some apple carts. We humans often entrust our lives to each other, but we make the assumption that wild animals, even other primates, do not.

To find baboons we took a Land Rover into the bush (there are too many lions in that region of Kenya to walk), where I sometimes encountered the Masai walking about. I'd ask them to direct me to the creatures, and they occasionally served as guides. This was how I became familiar with the Masai, and the ways in which they cared for and groomed each other.

Apart from the obvious utility of such grooming after long days spent in the bush, the pair bonds and the parent-child bonds of the Masai were preserved and strengthened by it (and it was by watching the Masai that I realized what a shame it is that we in the so-called developed countries lack both the leisure and the inclination to emulate the grooming practice more than just occasionally).

When I was actually observing baboons, it was best not to have Masai around, however. They made the baboons skittish, for the animals recognized the Masai as the people who ran them off their grazing land. Mike and I observed the primates alone, from our Land

Rover, at a great enough distance so as not to disturb the groups of ten to a hundred baboons that crossed the savannah. When they paused, beneath a shade or fruit tree, anywhere from two to eight pairs would begin grooming. They groomed for the same reasons the Masai did, to remove burrs and insects from each other's fur. The grooming seemed to take place, as others before me had already established, between animals closely related. We were able to see for ourselves an adult's vigilance while it groomed a baby, and the converse as well; the adult being groomed by another adult was the one scanning the horizon.

This whole line of inquiry had been sparked by Tiko's ardent reverie around my hands and hair as I rose from sleep.

"All right," I'd say to Tiko, after about ten minutes of allopreening, "it's time to start the day." He would climb onto my hand and I would carry him upstairs to the office for our morning feeding. We had working breakfasts. The perfect gentleman, he'd wait on his perch for me to dig into my cereal, grapefruit, bananas, other fruit, before picking at his own repast of lettuce, fruit, Cheerios, and milk.

Parrots in the wild share Tiko's gentility. This may be because they have to lower their heads to eat, which makes them vulnerable to predators. The flock is better defended when feeding in a group, with the birds on the perimeter keeping watch. Tiko's table manners also indicated that he wanted to be assured that his mate had sufficient food. If Mike brought Tiko a snack, with a little something for himself, but left me out, Tiko wouldn't touch it. I'd have to have several mouthfuls of whatever Mike was eating (there was no way to fake it) before Tiko dipped his beak into food. The exception was Chinese food, which Tiko quickly learned I would rarely touch. If Mike placed a little of his Chinese takeout on Tiko's yellow plate, the bird dug right in, never mind that I was still waiting for my pizza to warm up.

After breakfast, I'd settle in to work, and Tiko would stand upon his perch, preening, sleeping, and watching for predators out the window, since I was clearly slacking in my vigilance duties. He was delighted when I proofread, because I then had one hand free to preen him.

IN DUE COURSE it came to my attention that the bird was musty, and spreading fine flakes of dander through the house. Many newly hatched chicks are covered, or partially covered, in down feathers, which in most species are soon replaced by contour feathers covering the head and body, along with wing and tail feathers. Unlike most other birds, adult parrots retain their down feathers, the barbs of which continually disintegrate into a fine powder. Parrots use this powder to clean the rest of their plumage, the way campers might use dry leaves or sand to clean a pot when there is no soap or water about. It is this powder that gives their feathers their characteristic whitish bloom. Egrets, too, have powder down, which they use to remove dirt and oil from their feathers to keep them an immaculate white.

Whenever Tiko shook himself or fluffed up his feathers, the powder flew everywhere. You could see it drifting through the shafts of sunlight. I was particularly aware of his dander when I worked on my computer. The static electricity drew the pale white powder to the screen.

Things became worse when he began to molt. The new body feathers grew in covered by tiny, translucent sheaths, and when these fell off they commingled with the powder down. Some people are seriously allergic to all this "dust" and are laid low by their molting birds. But Mike and I were lucky, afflicted by only a sneeze or two.

In the tropics, frequent heavy rains send wild parrots scurrying under thick coverings of leaves. The rain gently penetrates the leaves, dribbling down onto the birds, which emerge after such a storm has passed glistening wet and clean. Parrots living in deserts bathe in sand, using it much like powder down. They use the same bathing motions as do parrots in water, getting the sand all over their bodies to pull off the dirt, dust, and oil. Sand also removes lice and other vermin caught in their feathers. Either way, the feathers are cleansed of the disintegrating feather sheaths and excess oil, dirt, and other debris that prevent the barbules of each feather from forming an interlocking unit. Bathing humidifies the respiratory passages (they have a trachea, just like us, as well as air passages in the bones) and sinuses as well; this is especially important for parrots in captivity, when excessive heating during cold winters makes houses particularly dry.

So it was that one warm spring day I determined that it was time for Tiko to have a bath.

"Sweetheart," I said, "it's time for a bath!" He cocked his head and looked at me in a funny way. Did he know what I was saying, or did my tone alert him to the fact that we were about to try something new? In any event, I clearly sensed that he knew something was afoot. When I held out my arm, there was a momentary hesitation before he let me convey him to the bathroom and place him on the sink's edge. He gingerly lifted up one foot and then the other, as though unsure of the slippery porcelain surface; he ruffled his feathers slightly and emitted a low warbling sound from deep in his throat. Perhaps the nearby toilet, into which he had plunged so ignominiously upon first arriving in his new abode, was also a factor into what was clearly his growing discomfort. In the confines of the bathroom his musty malodorous scent was particularly strong.

"Parrots like to bathe," I reassured him. "We want you to be a sweet-smelling bird!"

He crooned softly to me, then became silent, following my every move. I filled the plant spritzer with warm water. He glared at it with suspicion.

"Just relax," I told him. "This will be fun!"

The first burst of mist from the spritzer provoked squawks of displeasure; at the second, he screeched, awkwardly glided to the floor (for he was still in midmolt), and hightailed it down the hall as fast as his stubby little legs could carry him. He looked at me balefully for the rest of the day.

"That bird smells," Guy quipped at dinner that night. "Can't you give him a bath?"

I told him I couldn't even get Tiko with the spritzer.

"See, I told you he was neurotic. Who ever heard of a rain forest bird that was afraid of water?"

"He may be afraid of water because he fell in the toilet when he first came here and nearly drowned." When Guy heard this he couldn't quite repress an impish grin.

I bravely forged on. "A good soak can chill a bird, make it sick, even kill it from hypothermia. The toilet might have awakened in him an instinctual fear of water."

"A classic phobic response," said Guy in the mock German accent of an analyst. "Neurosis, as I said."

We all had to laugh. But the laughter did not quite erase the concern I felt at the truth of his words.

I had a similar result with Tiko a few days later, when, once again, assaulted by his smell, I tried to take him with me into the shower. "I'll hold you near the spray and just mist you, get your feathers wet," I told him. "You know parrots are rain forest birds. Who ever heard of a rain forest bird who doesn't like to get wet?" I was distressed to find that I was parroting Guy.

With what was obviously trepidation (squawks and a futile, half-hearted flapping of wings) the brave fowl hopped onto my arm. He came with me into the bathroom, but then, as soon as I turned on the shower, he flopped unceremoniously to the floor and waddled away.

None of my tactics changed his attitude. He would follow me to the bathroom while I showered (like he followed me everywhere else). But he made sure to wait for me at a safe distance outside the door.

After his molt, as the worst of the dander dispersed, his smell diminished somewhat. Whenever he saw the mister in my hand, he would fly to his highest perch on the bookshelves in the living room and stay there until I had finished spritzing the many plants we have around the house.

Tiko's aversion to water and his trauma around his dunk in the loo reminded me of two baby parakeets I had rescued that had become completely waterlogged in a torrential downpour. Mike and I were on Costa Rica's Osa Peninsula, observing parrots and their habitat. We took up residence in a cozy little lodge.

One night, a spectacular storm rolled through. We watched as walls of black clouds laced with lightning swept across the bay at dusk. For about an hour we were deluged by rain. Following such a storm, most birds will spend hours preening oil into their feathers, which keeps the feathers intact so that cold rain does not penetrate to the skin. Until very recently, the predominant view among biologists was that feathers evolved in the first place as a way to insulate the body and help maintain a constant body temperature, rather than as an aid to flight (just as mammals evolved hair). Feathers, so the theory went, were used only secondarily for gliding, and still later for full flight.

Most scientists believe that feathers evolved from reptilian scales—but just which reptile was the ancestor of modern birds is in dispute. In 1970, John Ostrom of Yale University published research that argued that birds had probably evolved from dinosaurs. That view prevailed in the scientific community until the recent discovery of Longisquama, a small, odd-looking reptile, which glided among the trees in central Asia 220 million years ago, around the time of the appearance of the first dinosaurs and 75 million years before Archaeopteryx, long considered the first bird. Longisquama was covered in what appear to be feathers. It also had a wishbone, which provides a place for the attachment of the strong breast muscles necessary for flight, suggesting that similar muscles were present in Longisquama.

Is Longisquama the ancestor of modern birds? The scientists who made the discovery are careful not to make this claim, although Terry D. Jones, a member of the discovery team, is quite certain they've found the earliest feather. But the small reptile does seem to be a likely candidate. My view is, let's wait and see what other evidence comes to light.

The find has also cast another shadow on generally accepted wisdom. Alan Feduccia of the University of North Carolina, an ornithologist who has long held out against the birds-as-modern-day-dinosaurs theory, believes that Longisquama might do more than establish a new reptilian ancestor for birds; he argues that the structure of its hollow shafts covered by sheaths indicates that the initial function of feathers was not to provide insulation but for flight. If this proves accurate, it would be a truly exciting discovery. Flight feathers are a remarkable adaptation, and the story of their development has long been a mystery.

Mike and I saw the weakness of wet feathers as insulation when we walked out into the garden of our Costa Rican lodge after that big storm passed. Every leaf and petal, every vine, was drenched, so we decided to walk around the grounds rather than into the forest. It was drizzling, and the air was very cool. We heard an eerie, mewing sound, and left the path to search out its source in the vegetation nearby. Our flashlights illuminated two small bedraggled parrots, in the lower branches of a cashew tree with bright red fruits, whimpering softly. They were so rumpled and wet they hardly resembled what they were, although closer inspection revealed them to be Orange-chinned Parakeets. They were fledglings, too young to be out of their nest and away from their parents; they had not yet learned to seek cover in a storm. I reached to one and then the other. They both stepped willingly onto my hand, and clung to it tightly as we made our way back to the lodge.

Back in the room, I rolled them around in a dry towel, while they moaned softly. As they warmed up they began ferociously preening. Mike and I put them just inches from my pillow. They grasped the brass spokes of the headboard with their tiny claws. The heavy rains returned that night and continued until dawn. The birds were unlikely to have survived had they remained outside.

In the morning I was awakened by both of them preening my hair. They clearly wanted to be friends. I learned later that they were "wild" pets of the innkeeper, and regularly roosted at night in a cashew tree. Their parents may have been killed by predators, or, more likely, the kids at the lodge had pilfered the chicks from their nest.

For the rest of our stay, the birds descended from the trees when I called out. "What are you doing, kids?" I'd say, and they'd scurry down through the branches to perch happily on my hand. Sometimes they would scramble to my shoulder and ride there when Mike and I went into the jungle. I was told that mine was the only voice they responded to. It was as though the two little ones knew that I had saved their lives that cold night in the storm.

Their cute antics made me miss Tiko all the more. I grew close to them and hated to leave, but I knew the people at the lodge would care for them, and the children loved them. The last day I carried them everywhere, and in the evening tenderly returned them to the branches of their favorite tree.

"Good-bye, my little ones," I said, choking up. "Please be careful. Don't let yourselves get too wet and cold."

When one gently touched his beak to my lips, I had to turn and walk away. It was hard enough. I didn't want to burden them with my tears.

SHOWERS ASIDE, TIKO BECAME, that summer after we bonded, remarkably compliant (at least within certain perimeters). I had a special stick, about a half inch in diameter and eighteen inches long, which I would present him with before Mike and I left for work at eight-thirty in the morning. It signaled that it was time for him to return to his cage. Mike and I had taken to leaving sticks in every room so that one was always handy should the bird become foul-tempered.

I didn't want Tiko to associate stepping onto my hand with returning to his cage, so I always used the stick to take him there. He didn't dislike his cage; quite the contrary. Nevertheless, I made certain to offer him my hand only when we were about to do something I thought he might enjoy. The summer progressed nicely. Mike and I stayed close to home, forgoing our customary research jaunts to the far corners of the world. I spent my time in my lab at Rutgers. The school was quiet during the summer months. I worked with a few assistants, in the field with Mike, or at home, writing articles for academic journals. I puttered about in the garden. All in all it was a pleasant change of pace from my normally frenetic schedule. It was nice to slow down, to be at home for an extended period of time.

In the fall, when I went back to teaching, Tiko was never far from my thoughts. His bond to me was a responsibility of which I was constantly aware. It did not feel like a burden, rather a kind of pact or trust that I was proud to fulfill. The days grew shorter, the sun paled, and light leaked from the sky. Tiko and I were approaching our first anniversary. When I was with him, I watched him constantly with more than mere doting appreciation or intellectual curiosity. His behaviors were highly suggestive. I had begun to see that he had a great deal to teach me.

Although Amazons are widespread in the tropics and some species are common, their behavior and breeding habits are largely unknown in the wild. They are difficult to observe through the dense tropical vegetation, and they tend to nest in cavities near the tops of trees. Most of their activities take place in the canopy, and their shifting shades of green merge with the vines and leaves of the forest. I've spent hour upon hour watching an Amazon nesting hole in Costa Rica, to be rewarded only by a brief sighting of a visiting male. When they aren't breeding, the flock flies long distances between their roosts and feeding trees. They are quite noisy when they fly but silent when they feed, and it's a lot easier to hear them than to see them in all the greenery.

After they have fed, they may sit for hours (as Tiko does at home), resting motionless in the treetops. They resemble the flowers and fruits swaying in the breeze; you hardly know they're there. Some sleep while others preen. Pairs often preen each other, bill (touch bills), coo, and snuggle.

Tiko kept to the same schedule. He usually quieted after his morning meal, dozing in his cage after we departed. Some popular authors on the care of pet parrots claim that this is a difficult time for the bird. One suggestion they offer is that the owner ring up the parrot during the day, and perhaps leave a "Hello, love!" on the answering machine, so the parrot can hear it. My considered opinion is that there is no need for this. But to cover my tracks I told Tiko that in a pinch he was free to call me. So far, he hasn't.

Our work schedule seemed to appeal to him. If Mike and I happened to stay home on a weekday, around midday Tiko would fly down from our bright sunlit office to the railing outside the bedroom, where it was darker, tuck his bill in his back feathers, and sleep for an hour or two, just as he did on weekends. This gave him a few extra hours in the middle of the day to rest up for the evening's activities. Parrots are perfectly able to adjust to a complicated schedule, I am convinced, so long as they know what it is. Our routine soon became Tiko's, and he clung to it fiercely. He preferred waking up at the same time every day (although this shifts slightly as the days grow longer), even if I happened to rise earlier than usual. Should I be late for a meal, he'd fly to his perch or call out "Crackerboy!" to remind me that it was time for us to eat.

Over time Tiko adjusted to our routines and came to anticipate our every move. When I picked up my briefcase in the morning, he'd fly to the railing and wait for me to fetch the stick. He'd been up late with us, after all, and had no objection to catching a few winks now.

Wild parrots get a lot of sleep—the whole night (twelve hours in equatorial regions), plus an hour here or there during the day.

Once in a great while, on a busy morning, I'd forget to put him in his cage before I left the house. When I returned in the evening he'd be sitting in it anyway, the cage door wide open. If we slipped up, it was his job to enforce the routine. Some parrots feel banished to their cages and come to dislike them, but for Tiko it was his refuge. He would remain in it even after I returned from work, until I offered him my hand. If I were slow to arrive he would summon me loudly, often by giving his blaring contact call, but he did so from his cage. He was reinforcing my training. My role was to appear, put my fingers on the bars, wait for him to nibble them, then reach in and take him out. Any departure from that sequence of events upset him.

He taught me how not to be bitten, which, once I got the hang of it, was simple enough: learn what provoked him and do not repeat it. Since parrots are small compared to cats and dogs, we expect to be able to approach them and cart them around as we please. I certainly had this notion when Tiko first joined us. Yet we would not presume to pick up a cat every time we felt the urge. Parrots, Tiko insisted, should be treated with equal respect.

IT WAS IN THE COURSE of our second year together that I felt Tiko was fully integrated into his new home. He sometimes lunged or nipped when he was hungry, or overtired, or when he woke in the morning or was woken in the middle of the night. He detested surprises: a new experience could trigger a hostile attitude, or worse.

But he grew less anxious, less apt to cross swords with Mike and me. As I learned to read his signs, and as he came to understand that he was here to stay, he nipped and squawked less frequently. It was a moot question whether I had trained him or he had trained me. I suspected the latter. I was the one who'd had to learn to read his body language, to fathom the meaning of his calls and sounds.

Corporal punishment turned me into a good pupil. I learned that a slight dip of the head meant he didn't want to go somewhere, and that a series of soft coos meant: "Please take me with you." I came to distinguish a hostile lunge, in which the neck and bill are pointed downward, from the desire to approach, in which the neck and bill are held straight. I knew beyond a shadow of a doubt what it meant when his eyes flashed bright red, and I became alert to the crisp, rasping call that accompanied certain of his lunges. But there was something else occurring along with my growing proficiency. The signals themselves had become clearer. His early ambivalence had made them muddy and hard to read. Once he grew certain of what he wanted, he turned into the Great Communicator. If I pestered him when he was in one of his Greta Garbo moods, I would pay for it with a nip, but rarely one that drew blood. Following such a skirmish, he would flash his eyes at me, as if to say, "I made my meaning clear, why are you so obtuse?"

But mostly he was content to hang out and keep an eye on me, and engage in some serious allopreening. He spent a lot of time asleep beside me, or clinging to my hand or leg. He particularly seemed to enjoy holding on to my foot as I stood in the closet, choosing an outfit in the morning.

This is how parrots are: not only are they deeply attached to their flock, they're homebodies. Even when they fly long distances from their roosts to feeding trees, they always return to the roost at night. (The exceptions are a few species, living in the arid interior of Australia, that are nomads, moving across hundreds of miles of new terrain each day in search of food and water.)

I was keenly aware of and grateful for the rare glimpses Tiko gave me into the world of birds, the opportunity to observe behaviors I would have never been able to see in the wild. In the new environment he had come to accept, I was his companion, not some unfamiliar creature against whom he had to be on guard. The richness of his world gradually opened to me. He kept me apprised of my ignorance, my limited understanding of the lives of birds.

Nor would it be extravagant to say that over the course of that first year Tiko subtly altered the direction of my career. He redirected my interests from pure science to that place where science and wildlife management intersect. I saw that my responsibility to him, the trust in which he held me, extended to all creatures and the planet as a whole. Tiko was my catalyst for this. I had been interested in preserving the coastal beaches of my beloved terns and skimmers; now I wanted to look at the ways we might preserve the habitat of animals around the world.

Winter passed and we were into the spring when Tiko, too, donned new regalia. He molted for the second time, and his wing feathers dropped symmetrically. When they regrew, their colors were almost impossibly bright.

6

Tiko Is No Birdbrain

BECAUSE OF OUR HECTIC SCHEDULES, MIKE AND I RARELY found the time for a leisurely breakfast, not even on weekends or holidays. But one Sunday morning in April 1989, about a year after Tiko had bonded with me, I decided to alter the pattern. The sun warmed us through the window facing the garden; daffodils spiked through the snow. Finches and woodpeckers were making good use of the feeder. I was married to a good, gentle man. My relationship with Tiko had continued to mature, and I had the feeling that sometimes occurs, out of the blue, that everything is right with the world.

"Let's dawdle over breakfast," I suggested.

"What for?"

"To celebrate being together. We're wonderfully suited, and I love you now more than ever."

He cocked an eyebrow. "Sounds like a plan."

"Let's enjoy the spring. Let's watch the competition among the squirrels."

This may not sound like a big date to you, but for two field biologists it was better than a night at the opera.

"Fine by me," said Mike. "I've always had a weakness for squirrels."

Tiko glided in and joined us in the dining nook. He flew to his perch by the window and watched his fellow birds feeding in the garden. I put homemade strawberry jam (a gift from my sister Barbara) on the table, hot biscuits, warm bagels, cream cheese, and smoked salmon. Tiko had always eaten in his own space, and, as usual, I piled his yellow plate high with Cheerios, lettuce, and fruit. Then I smeared cream cheese on two bagel halves and handed one to Mike. As I took my first bite, Tiko abandoned his birdy repast and scampered across the window ledge, climbed onto the table, and marched over to my plate. His eyes darted from my bagel to my face. When I didn't scold him or shoo him away, he leaned down and peeled a bit of cream cheese from the bagel. It vanished swiftly down his throat. He looked at me and flashed his eyes. I got the message: Now we're talking FOOD; you've been holding out on me, Joanna, enough of this eating like a bird.

From then on Tiko ate what I did, and not from his dish but my own. His tastes were eclectic, often ethnic. He became an amusing and involved dinner companion. Along with plates, napkins, glasses, knives, and forks there would be Tiko, waiting expectantly, part of the table setting. During dinner he'd browse, peering at our plates and the serving dishes containing sundries more or less to his liking, looking for something interesting to try. Between courses, he'd wipe his beak clean of sticky foods—pudding, for instance—by rubbing it against the table's edge. When I'd try to wipe his bill with a napkin, he'd become indignant. "No! No! No!" he'd squawk. With time, we made it a game. I'd try to wipe his bill while he tried to wrest the napkin from my hand.

Pudding, pasta, corn on the cob, sweet potatoes, chicken—he had a taste for them all. It wasn't chicken meat he seemed to want so much as the bones. He would grab a denuded drumstick in his right foot, crack it with a single bite, split the shaft, and extract its marrow with his tongue.

You rarely find behaviors in captivity that do not also exist in the wild, and while no one has ever seen a wild parrot gnawing on a bone, my surmise is that they would if given half a chance. Many herbivores will eat meat when they have the opportunity. On a visit to China in 1992, I found to my surprise that scientists trapping pandas would bait the cage with goat meat rather than bamboo, which everyone knows is the staple of the panda's diet. Many more animals eat carrion than we think.

It was long believed that our closest primate relatives were vegetarians. Jane Goodall discovered that chimps eat meat, and that they even form hunting parties to attack and kill their prey—often a young member of another troop. Parrots, however, are scavengers rather than hunters. Because they spend nearly all their time in treetops, they're unlikely to come across carcasses of other animals. But I can imagine a bird dying in a nest cavity, its bone marrow providing a nutritious snack for the parrot who found it.

Anthropologists suggest that nutrition-packed marrow from the bones of antelopes and wildebeests killed and discarded by lions and leopards helped early humans survive on the African plains. Bones from early digs in Africa contain both predator teeth marks, and, superimposed, the hack marks of primitive knives. Our ancestors might have hidden in the bush while a large beast killed its quarry. Once the lion or leopard abandoned the kill, early man moved in and dragged the bones back to his cave. Were I to find myself transported to the African plain, I'd choose to run the vultures off a lion kill rather than hunt down a gazelle. The vultures would be feisty, but I'd only have to keep them at bay for a moment.

One of the advantages of scavenging for food was that women, too, could find meat. Scavenging calls into question the theory that men's strength and aggressiveness evolved from hunting. If these traits didn't come from hunting, where did they come from? For what were they used? Is male dominance—physically, economically, and politically—relatively recent, masquerading as an ancient, immutable trait? Recorded history is ten thousand years old, compared to the over 4-million-year period man and his ancestors have walked the earth. The social behavior of Homo sapiens could have been very different for much of our evolution.

TIKO, TOO, WAS A SCAVENGER, cracking open the chicken bones on my plate. It was share and share alike at the table, and this new arrangement seemed to be a tangible manifestation of how, in what I now think of as our "middle period," the balance of power between us shifted. I stopped treating Tiko like a pet. I began to see him as an autonomous creature whose dependence on me only highlighted the need to really understand, deep down, that his life was as important as mine, his desires and inclinations equally valid. It was he who had been transposed, forced to adapt, live in the world of these strange creatures who slept in beds, spoke mostly in gibberish, ate with forks and knives, and, worst of all, took showers. He trained me well. I came to know that the contest of wills between me and the parrot who owned me was beside the point. It was obvious who was lord of our roost.

Of course, I can confess to you (although I would never do so in front of Tiko) that it was not only appreciation for the intrinsic dignity of all life that caused me to indulge Tiko. To casual visitors he may have appeared to be a spoiled child, with me doing the spoiling. Was he a petty tyrant? Did Mike and I cower in the face of his moods? Perhaps. But Tiko was also furthering my scientific career, and if you know anything about me by this point, it is that I would go to extremes to make new scientific discoveries. I have already mentioned that watching Tiko had subtly redirected my career into the arena of public policy and to not so subtly suggest research topics. He now also began to widen my understanding of bird behavior.

Somewhat late in the day, I began to use my scientific training to unravel Tiko's mysteries, and as he came clear so did hitherto unexplained parrot behavior, as well as the behavior of other birds I had studied. Tiko made me pay attention to details that otherwise would have gone unnoticed. I began by correlating his behavior to behavior I had observed in the wild. What I had assumed to be orneriness on his part turned out to have, under this kind of scrutiny, a wild counterpart. For example, his habit of eating one kind of food and one kind only for days or weeks on end, and then quite suddenly refusing to eat it at all, had been especially vexing, until I figured out its source. In nature, most flowers, seeds, fruits, and nuts are available for only a few days or weeks. So a wild parrot will eat figs, and only figs, when figs are ripe. When the fig trees are exhausted, the bird must switch, say, to cashew fruit. Tiko was replicating the foraging habits of his wild ancestors.

Once this was clear to me I was better able to tolerate his gastronomic quirks. And I never raised objection to his eating from my plate, although this "sharing" was far from reciprocal. While most of my Tiko-inflicted scars date from our earliest time together, the one on the back of my left hand is the result of an absentminded grab for a couple of peanuts from his yellow plate, which, I discovered the hard way, was off-limits at this point in our relationship, even to me. Tiko changed in time, and showed extraordinary instances of generosity and selflessness (his courtship regurgitation of pinyon nuts on my hand is a case in point), but these were still relatively early days, and I did not yet see the signs of his incipient largesse.

GENERALLY I WAS WILLING to condone and tease out meaning, rather than condemn. But when it came to my fresh hibiscus blooms, I tried to draw the line. Tiko climbed among the branches, biting off flowers and eating just the base of each. I reasoned with him: "Sweetie, don't do that. Those pretty flowers are meant for looking at. Come, Tiko, why not eat this?" I pointed at his yellow dish, piled high with fresh fruit and vegetables. He glanced at me, an oddly curious glance that was full of the implacable will of the parrot. "Why do you even bother wasting your breath?" it seemed to say. Then he resumed his quest for the next hibiscus bloom. It would have been less troubling had he eaten the whole flower, but he bit off a bloom only to snack on its nectar-rich base.

Attempts to stop him would be useless. Parrots in Costa Rica eat the flowers, along with the fruits, of many trees. Among their favorites are Wild Papaya, *Fruta de Mono* (Monkey Fruit), and *Huevos de Caballo* (Horse Balls). They fling away flower after flower, just as Tiko did, once they have consumed the nectar. For some parrots, like the Scaly-headed Amazon in Brazil, flowers make up 20 to 40 percent of their diet.

Tiko also found my roses, nasturtiums, bee balm, and mints to his liking. He ate the bright yellow and purple pansies my brother Roy had given us. Lilies, too, were a favorite. He stood beside a vase, stretched up his neck, grabbed hold of a lily stem, and backed away from the vase, wresting the flower to the table. In the end I let him eat whatever he wanted. It was next to impossible to have a decent bouquet of lilies anyway; the deer ate the best ones long before I could get them from the garden to the house, then Tiko polished off the rest.

ALMOST FROM THE DAY he arrived, Tiko had begun chewing on our wooden window moldings. "You can't do that," I'd say, cajole or coerce him onto my finger, and carry him to his perch. But he kept returning to the sill to chew its wood. If I persisted in removing him he'd lunge and sometimes nip my hand. If I brought the stick, he would usually step onto it and bite *it* in frustration. Many a parrot has been banished permanently to its cage for wood chewing, although in one sense we were lucky, since more than a few of them prefer furniture to window frames.

We hit on a solution quite by accident. We were building Tiko a new perch with apple wood we'd pruned from one of our trees. We attached the apple wood to a heavy steel base, so that he could fly to and from his perch without mishap. Only moments after he discovered the new perch he began chewing on its bark, and actually swallowed some. He spent hours loosening, dislodging, and eating bits of bark, and completely lost interest in the moldings. From then on we made sure he always had a tasty log on which to chew.

I made it a point to look for similar habits in wild Red-lored Amazons. In Costa Rica, I watched them pull bark from trees and eat it. The activity, in fact, took up a good portion of their time. They sidled along branches, looking for promising spots, then loosened the wood with their bills. Eventually, working also with their feet, they'd yank off a chunk, hold it in their claws, and chew. Some wood would be discarded, but they got most of it down. They would hang upside down, if they had to, to get at a particularly fetching piece. The bark no doubt served to hone their bills, which continue to grow, like the claws of a cat, and need to be regularly shortened and sharpened.

The bark provides roughage in a diet that otherwise consists largely of flowers and fruit. It may also contain nutrients necessary for a healthy parrot diet, or provide grit, tiny bits of crushed material that help grind up food in a parrot's gizzard, a thickened muscular pouch in the intestinal tract just before the stomach.

Another of Tiko's perplexing behaviors, on which my Costa Rica trip shed light, was his need for hourly attention. He would chat me up from a distance, in his garbled squawking, or else come up close and ask to be preened. I much too readily assumed that such habits resulted from his insecurities, and I was mystified when they continued long after it should have become clear to him that we were stuck with each other for life. But after I had watched Red-lored Amazons in the wild, over the course of many trips, several things became clear. During much of the year they feed in small flocks, moving from tree to tree. Sometimes, as I watched, they would sail noisily over the forest, as if summoning, by their clamor, other members of the flock. At other times they would pass unseen—unless I happened to be watching the sky—in utter silence over the forest canopy, the mated pairs flying near one another. The pairs remained in close proximity after the flock settled in a tree and began to feed.

Every half hour or so, one member of a mated pair would clamber across the branch, never mind what edible fruit might lie between them, and sidle closer to its mate. Then, on cue, they would begin to preen each other, pecking delicately at the back and neck feathers of the other. These allopreening sessions lasted only long enough for the birds to feel that all was well. Then they each went back to feeding on the fruit.

Tiko, it might be said, carried this tendency to an extreme. He was content to preen with me for fifteen minutes or longer. This was probably related to the safety of his food supply, secure from competitors, always in view from his perch across the room.

I BEGAN TO FEEL an uncanny rapport with Tiko: pet, companion, handy source of scientific study—he was all these things, yet more; he had become my secret sharer, able to anticipate my moods, my next remark, my next act, just as I had come to feel eerily attuned to him, a dear, close friend and a sacred charge.

I developed insight, too, into the depth of his intelligence. One evening, while making dinner, I heard him cooing in the hallway. I left the kitchen and found him perched on the railing at the bottom of the stairs. He looked at me intently. I returned the gaze, perplexed. I offered him my hand. He let me carry him into the kitchen, and I placed him on the counter and went back to chopping garlic. But while I was at the sink washing vegetables, he disappeared. Again I heard his coos.

I returned to the hallway. What was the creature up to, perched at the bottom of the stairs? This time he declined my hand. He scrambled to the landing, shimmied up the banister post, and sat at the top of the railing. Was he leading me somewhere? Attuned to him or no, I couldn't, on that occasion, read his mind. I began to climb the stairs.

But he was already descending, sliding down the banister sideways, looking over his shoulder to see where he was headed. He grasped the banister much the way a person would, opposable toes hooked over the back, the others clenched around the front. He came at me a mile a minute. What if he didn't know how to stop? I started forward, but perilously close to the bottom post he tightened his grip and screeched to a stop. He glanced at me with pride and cooed.

"Tiko!" I clapped my hands. "That is terrific!"

From that point on, Mike and I often came upon him sliding down the railing, waddling back up, and sliding down again, enthralled by the game. Once he had shown me what he could do, he no longer needed an audience. The activity, needless to say, had no obvious purpose. He was playing. My surmise was that long before the night he summoned me to watch him strut his stuff, he had already learned that sliding down the banister was a way to reach me quickly, and only afterward did he discover that it was fun. In time he took to braking halfway down, finishing the trip in a more leisurely fashion. He was playing, yes, but also showing that he was in control.

The question of "play" in animals is an intriguing one. We use the word to connote activity that has no obvious use in daily life—almost a frivolous pastime. In fact, play has an important function for the animals that engage in it, humans included, and particularly for their young. It is a way of developing dexterity and motor coordination, and of discerning the boundaries of social behavior, both skills that are critical to success as an adult. Play, as we know from watching our children, is a form of learning. The correlation between intelligence and play has yet to be properly investigated. The chicken and egg conundrum would seem to apply: did the habit of play increase intelligence or did intelligence increase the need for play? The two more likely coevolved.

When we think of animals playing, the image that usually comes to mind is of frolicking young mammals—puppies wrestling, lion cubs nipping at each other. But intelligent birds such as parrots, crows, jays, and ravens engage in behavior we have to call play. Keas, those polygamous kidney-pecking, eyeball-eating parrots, are terrific players. They investigate unfamiliar objects with particular intensity. The delight they take in new things is wonderful to watch, although it often leads to mischief. They are captivated by bright and shiny things. I learned the hard way not to turn away from them with an open camera bag: I lost both lens caps and film. Their destruction of parked cars is joyous—they'll pry off shiny bits of chrome, even dislodge an antenna. I once watched a Kea slide down the curved back window of a car, repeating this feat over and over until he was joined by his friends.

Play is more common among the animals most at ease in their environment. Parrots, for example, who find all the food they'll need by midmorning, have plenty of time to hang out, whereas many other animals are stretched to the limit to find food and shelter. Young animals play more than adults partly because they're spared adults tasks. Parents provide food, shelter, and guard against danger, freeing up playtime for the young. Although Mike and I perform all these functions for Tiko, I imagine he did more playing at a younger age. I often think wistfully of a younger Tiko cavorting with his Florida ladies, and using his youthful charm and ebullience to push them around.

WILD PARROTS CAN LIVE for sixty or seventy years, and need to be able to adjust to a changing environment. Many of their forests have been converted to villages and farms. There is also uncertainty in their daily lives. They endure wet and dry seasons, hurricanes that destroy their feeding areas and nesting trees, and years during which there might be only a few fruiting trees. Temperate forests have perhaps a dozen common trees, but in the lowland tropical rain forests, which is where most parrots live, there are hundreds. Parrots come to learn the whereabouts of every fruiting tree, and to arrive at each during the few days of the year when its fruit is ripe.

This ability signifies intelligence of a high order. Learning may be defined, in fact, as how well an animal processes new information in order to be able to react to a changing environment. It is an adaptive change in behavior brought about by experience.

There are, of course, many creatures on the earth whose skillful use of their environment boggles the mind. Acacia ants have a symbiotic relationship with the Swollen-thorn Acacia trees of lowland Central America. The ants colonize the hollow thorns of the trees, which have evolved to provide them with the protein, oil, and sugar necessary for the survival of their colonies. The ants chase away grazers, mostly insects, that come to feed on the tree—thereby protecting their colony and the tree simultaneously. These trees cannot survive to reproductive maturity without the patrolling activities of a large acacia ant colony, and the ant colonies are never found anywhere outside the thorns of these trees. We don't think of ants as smart, even though they have adapted to and use their environment in remarkable ways. This is because their complex, instinctual behaviors have evolved over millions of years; but if part of their environment were to drastically change, or disappear, they would be out of luck. The intelligent animal, however, learns to adapt.

So if parrots are so adaptable, why are they fiends for order? They'll go to the same watering hole, visit the same clay lick, return to the same roosting place, again and again. Perhaps their rage for order is not unlike our scheduled mealtimes, or weekends off. Do religion and ritual fill this deep need in the face of what are often our chaotic lives?

MEMORY IS ANOTHER SIGN of intelligence, and Tiko's is extraordinary. If the peanut jar is empty, he'll make his way to the corner of the kitchen where we used to keep the nuts before we remodeled the room. If, from his perch behind my desk, he happens to observe that Mike has left his desk drawer open, he'll scurry over to look for pencils, although, for just that reason, we removed them years ago.

The memory of his humiliating fall into the toilet bowl will, apparently, remain with him for life. Years after the incident, I recall an occasion when I tried to put him on the toilet seat (with the lid down) while I retrieved some books from the edge of the bathtub. But he wouldn't leave my hand; in fact, he climbed up my arm to the safety of my shoulder.

Young parrots in the wild often remain with their parents long after they can go off on their own; it is wiser to stay, learn survival skills, commit to memory what they can. They watch their parents open seeds and fruits, and then they do the same. They learn from siblings and, since they are trained in groups, from playmates as well. I've watched family groups of Red-lored Amazons in Costa Rica moving slowly from tree to tree, remaining in contact by means of frequent calls. Thus, even after the young leave the nest, family members in a flock often travel together. It is usually assumed that when parrots are seen preening flock members not their mates, and not nestlings, the animals being preened are family members: grown offspring or siblings. But no one knows for sure, and no one, as far as I can tell, is exploring the issue.

There are many questions of this nature, and not enough people seeking answers. The conventional wisdom, which I share, is that parrots and their offspring maintain relationships for years. If this is so, then observational learning—learning by watching more experienced birds—is of the utmost importance to the education of young birds. This would at least partially explain the difficulties the U.S. Fish and Wildlife Service faced in its captive breeding program for Thick-billed Parrots.

These parrots disappeared from the United States in the 1930s, although some can still be found in the mountains of Mexico. While a few scattered high-elevation forests still exist in Arizona, the large forest tracts that once stretched into their Mexican territory are gone. But now, with the bird endangered in the forests of Mexico, periodic tries are made to reintroduce it to the Arizona mountains.

Such projects are inherently problematic. One can either reintroduce animals raised in captivity, or move wild animals to a new region. Both are iffy propositions; it is hard to teach animals raised in captivity to use a wild environment, and wild animals have already adapted to a specific region from which the new place will almost surely differ in dramatic ways. In either instance, there may be competitors in place who will outperform the newcomers. The attempt by the U.S. Fish and Wildlife Service to reintroduce Thick-billed Parrots failed largely because the birds, raised in captivity, could not be taught to feed on their traditional foods. Without parents or siblings to watch and imitate, they seemed not to know what to do. The scientists involved in the project valiantly pulled pinecones from branches, opened them up, and showed the birds the tasty seeds within. They may have even, with feigned enthusiasm, forced down a few. But the birds regarded them quizzically. They never did get the hang of it. When introduced to the wild, survival was low and reproduction didn't occur.

TIKO'S ADAPTABILITY, penchant for play, and memory are all signs of his intelligence. So, I think, is his dexterity. Parrots have opposable toes, two each in front and back, and their prehensile skills rival those of primates. This is as close as birds ever come to having hands. Parrots can cling to branches upright or upside down; they can use their feet to eat nuts, seeds, or M&M's. Other birds, such as raptors, carry fish, snakes, mice, and whatever else they kill in their talons. They're able to clutch and tear at things, but can no more manipulate objects than could a person without thumbs. Tiko picks up one cornflake at a time, brings each to his mouth, and nibbles genteelly. You could bring him to a White House dinner party without fear of embarrassment. Granted he might never learn to juggle tenpins while riding a unicycle, but what he does accomplish with his opposable digits is impressive.

For a long while scientists believed that intelligence evolved independent of form. A creature that walked on four limbs might evolve into one who walked on two, while its problem-solving capabilities developed entirely separately. A problem arose, you solved it, you lived longer than those who failed, you produced more offspring than those who failed, many of whom inherited your smarts and passed them on. Today, it is generally recognized that intelligence and form evolved side by side. Evolutionary biologists, for example, attribute the expansion of our brain to the development of the opposable thumb, which made it possible for our ancestors to manipulate and explore their environment. There's no evolutionary advantage to a large brain if you lack the physical means of implementing your big ideas. You might comprehend how useful making fire would be, you might know that good things would happen if you planted some seeds, but what good would that do if you couldn't strike the flint or dig the hole?

In human beings, curiosity and cognition presumably yielded new results when the prehensile thumb came along. In similar fashion, the development of opposable toes in parrots led to increased curiosity and greater development of the brain. Parrot neocortexes, the most advanced region of the brain, are larger in proportion to body size than that of most other birds.

Certain other birds are bright. Crows, for example, are skilled at adapting to people. They're quick to figure out that a scarecrow will do them no harm, and that someone with a gun is more dangerous than someone without. When I was a girl, the crows knew when I was on my way to chase them from the fields, and how long I'd stay once I got there. They would bide their time, keeping me in sight until I'd completed my rounds. Then they'd descend on our fields. But their feet limit them from eating foods with hard shells. They are nowhere near as dexterous, or as smart, as parrots.

I knew Tiko was smart, but I was shocked to see him use tools. When I was in graduate school, scientists took it for granted that human beings were the only tool users. Tool use, in fact, was considered to be one of the things that made us human. Other animals used objects, but they did not select a particular one for a particular task. Deer brushed against trees to mark a territory with pheromones. Wolves and dogs used trees or shrubs for a similar purpose, as scent posts, depositing urine as a warning. Many animals used trees, rocks, or other rough surfaces to scratch their bodies. Parrots used their discarded feathers as toys, flipping them about and pouncing on them. But obviously these were not tools. Tool use was a perquisite of human beings.

Then Jane Goodall found that chimps used sticks to fish insects out of holes in trees and stumps. If this wasn't tool use, what was it? News came that even birds used tools. Male Palm Cockatoos in Australia and northern New Guinea banged their feet on hollow logs to attract mates and warn competitors away from their territory. Then one day, some enterprising male birds were seen breaking off sticks to thump their hollow logs with, raising a racket far superior to feet alone. Tool use? You bet.

I've seen a Woodpecker Finch in the Galápagos use a thorn to pry grubs out of wood. The Egyptian Vulture will straddle an Ostrich egg it has just stolen, and repeatedly smash a rock against the hard shell. What are thorn and rock if not tools? Herring Gulls drop mussel or clam shells from a height onto the pavement to break them open. In this case, the question of tool use is less clear-cut. It can be said that the gulls are merely using their environment, not a particular device they have selected, in order to achieve the desired effect. But I would argue that the pavement, and the force of gravity, are being used as tools. In Barnegat Bay in central New Jersey I've seen young Herring Gulls watch adults drop shells from heights, crack the shells, and eat. You can almost hear the young ones saying, "Aha!" They take off with mussels in their beaks, drop them on sand, and nothing happens. They try again, from a greater height, and nothing happens. They next try dropping the shell onto a road, but if it turns out to be a dirt road, nothing happens. When the surface is concrete, they finally achieve results. Your enterprising gull will then figure out that he can break the shells open on a board. Should you, while beachcombing, come across a board surrounded by shells, you know you've seen the handiwork of an Einstein of a Herring Gull. But if you own a beach house, and the gulls are dropping shells onto your roof and car, your admiration will be tempered.

In the early 1970s, there was a legendary Green Heron in the National Zoo in Washington, D.C., who invented a fishing lure. The heron dropped a feather in the small brook that ran through his enclosure, then rushed downstream to spear any fish that rose to the bait. This tool-using bird entertained visitors for hours on end. I've watched herons in the wild do the same thing with sticks. In Japan, other herons use twigs, leaves, flies, and other insects for bait.

Although I was familiar with these stories, and had observed the truth of many of them firsthand, I was nonetheless astonished when Tiko used a tool for the first time. One morning, not long after he had begun to share my plate, he came over to solicit preening while I was busy at my desk.

"In a second, Tiko. Just let me wrap this up."

He persisted, poking at the fingers of one hand, then the other, tugging at my pen. In contests of this kind, Tiko usually had his way. But abruptly he straightened up and looked around. I could almost see him thinking. With determination, he waddled over to the bookcase and laboriously ascended to the shelf on which I kept his molted wing and tail feathers in a tall glass. I raptly watched as he took a feather in his beak, lifted it partway out, looked it over, and let it fall back into the glass. He did this again with another feather, and another. At last, a long primary feather passed inspection. He seized it firmly in his beak and reared up to remove it from the glass. I watched in awe as he transferred the feather to his right foot, with the quill pointing inward. Then he proceeded to scratch his head. He gently maneuvered the nub of the feather to and fro across his neck and face and, with particular care, around his eyes. He transferred the feather (via his bill) to his other foot, and he did his other side. His eyes closed and his head dropped until it touched the shelf. This was exactly how he responded when I preened him. But now he was lost in a swoon of autoerotic bliss.

Here was an example not just of tool use, but of what I call "insight learning." By this I mean the ability to solve a problem without first experimenting with possible solutions. For example, it wasn't as if Tiko had brushed up against a pencil and discovered through trial and error that he could use it to preen himself. He had conceptualized the problem and its solution, and I was blown away.

After that first time, Tiko would return to the glass jar whenever I was unresponsive to his overtures. He continued to solicit preening, and we continued to allopreen for the pleasure it gave us. The jar was his fallback position, his bonus to himself. I was fascinated to see autoeroticism in a creature other than primates.

Sometimes we'd try to have him demonstrate his tool-using prowess to company; we'd offer him a feather, and a hint or two of what to do with it. But like many a proud pet owner trying to show off his latest trick, Mike and I were often disappointed. If Tiko wasn't in the mood, he'd throw the feather to the floor. If we still missed his point, he'd flash his eyes.

Not long after his first autopreening session, Tiko found a way to save himself the journey to the jar. If a feather fell out while he was preening, he would use it to scratch himself. If he felt one coming loose, he'd pluck at it and help it on its way.

Then he discovered that a pencil could be used for scratching as well. You could even preen with it! Of course, this triggered a conflict between his unquenchable desire to devour the pencil and what was sometimes his equally strong compulsion to preen with it.

Tiko's use of feathers to scratch himself is not a behavior one is apt to observe in the wild. Most wild parrots have mates or family members available for allopreening, and the tool use Tiko exhibits may have no function in the jungle. But wild parrots spend most of their lives hidden in the high canopy: who knows what they do up there? Somewhere in Costa Rica there may well be an old widower Amazon with no family, obliged to rely on a feather or a stick to get at those hard-to-reach places.

There was another way in which Tiko's intelligence dazzled us. The Kama Sutra says one of the sixty-four tasks a man should master is teaching a parrot to talk. Central and South American tribes believed that, because of their capacity for speech, parrots have human souls. Queen Victoria had a pet parrot who greeted her each morning, to her great delight, with "God save the Queen!"

For thousands of years, parrots have astounded us with their ability to speak and understand our language. Until recently scientists thought this ability to be purely imitative, a thoughtless "parroting" of human speech. Recent research indicates that the cognitive and communicative abilities of birds have long been underestimated, especially those of parrots.

Based on her long-term research, Dr. Irene Pepperberg, of the ecology and evolutionary biology department of the University of Arizona, Tucson, and the author of *The Alex Studies: Cognitive and Communicative Abilities of Grey Parrots,* thinks that parrots process information at the level of chimpanzees and dolphins. Irene's African Grey Parrots talk about their likes and dislikes. Not only do they relate words to objects, but they also put together coherent sentences that express their needs and feelings. "I'm sorry, I wanna go back," said one of her birds when he realized she was about to leave him at the vet's.

Irene and I have been friends for twenty-five years, and I've made it a point to follow her research. She's been working with Alex, an African Grey she bought in a pet shop in Chicago in 1977. Alex can identify more than eighty objects, seven colors, and five shapes. He's learned some words on his own, including: paper, key, nut, wheat, truck, peg, wood, cork, corn, black, banana, pasta, rock, chair, popcorn, kiwi fruit, grain, carrot, cup, grape, and cherry, presumably from overhearing conversations and receiving rewards. When shown a three-cornered green piece of wood and asked, "What shape is it?" he will answer, "Three-cornered." When given objects of equal sizes but asked to pick out the biggest one, he will reply, "None."

Irene does not claim that Alex or her other experimental parrots know English; only that by training they have learned words and concepts, and that Alex can use these words to demonstrate comprehension and cognition. The difference is subtle, but it allows us to begin to understand how a parrot thinks, and what concepts and categories it can learn. George Page, in his delightful book *Inside the Animal Mind: A Groundbreaking Exploration of Animal Intelligence,* describes another of Alex's antics:

"As with many primates and mammals tested in lab conditions, boredom can be a problem with Alex. It is not rare for him to say in the middle of a test, 'I'm gonna go away,' and then do just that. But when he's engaged, he's tough to fool. When he says the word for a certain object, he cannot be tricked easily. For example, if Alex says 'wanna banana' and a nut is presented instead, one of three things will happen. He either refuses the nut in stony silence, refuses the nut and repeats his request for a banana, or accepts the nut and throws it at the conniving human being who had the nerve to try to trick him in the first place."

Critics point out that Irene has worked closely with Alex for over two decades—is she giving him subtle cues, of which she herself is perhaps unaware? Given the great care Irene has taken in designing her experiments, this attitude is clearly anthropocentric: some people simply do not want to believe that birds think. The same complaint could be made about the way children learn, after all. Parents interact closely with their kids for eighteen years. We do not expect to remove the "human" element from learning in children, or for children to learn without role models. Why should we expect other animals to learn this way? We send children to school for twelve years. Imagine what parrots could learn with the same level of instruction over a similar period of time!

Tiko, of course, has a limited spoken vocabulary (at least in English). He was a thirty-year-old bird when he came to me. Parrots, like people, pick up language when they're young, and Libby and Freda must not have made their bird's language acquisition a priority. I did not press him. His learning to speak in Somerset would have been like our trying to learn, as adults, another language by hearing only the words, with no written dictionary and no one to translate for us. He has continued, however, to pick up new sounds he hears around him.

Nonetheless, Tiko, as we have seen, is a skilled communicator. His jabbers, cackles, croons, screeches, and squawks clearly express his different moods and desires. Parrots are unique among animals in their vocal abilities. Most animal sounds are distinct notes, but parrots vocalize in complex tonalities, often sounding like more than one animal. Their calls are similar to the chants of Russian Tuva singers who produce a number of notes simultaneously by blowing air through constricted passages in their noses and throats.

Tiko does utter a few words clearly. "Hello!" issues from his cage whenever he wants to get out. Sometimes when he can't find us he waddles from room to room and screams, "Hello!" And "Wanna cracker!" and "Crackerboy!" echo through the house when he is in the mood for bread or crackers. Friends have told me that he occasionally says, "Joanna," but I don't hear it. And, of course, he's not shy about the use of the word "no!"

Tiko has a number of soliloquies that he does by rote, stringing endless series of phrases together. I am never sure if he is repeating snatches of the Yiddish he may have learned long ago in Florida, or snatches of programs he's heard on the radio. Once he starts a soliloquy, he repeats it from start to finish, staring soulfully into my eyes. My strong sense is that all of Tiko's calls, coos, and shrieks are some sort of communication—idle chitchat, sweet nothings, warnings of approaching doom. Mike and I have occasionally left a tape recorder running while we are away at work: Tiko remained silent throughout the day.

Tiko particularly likes to deliver soliloquies when I'm on the phone. He'll chatter and mew through whole conversations in his special phone voice, an incessant variation on a theme of about twenty syllables.

"All I can hear is the bird, Joanna." It's Guy.

"Tiko, honey, please," I tell him with mounting exasperation, "I'm on the phone." He pauses, cocks his head, and looks at me as if to say, "No kidding, you're on the phone? I hadn't noticed," and then resumes his jabber. Is he jamming me or just being social? He mimics my tone as the conversation winds down—he seems blessed with the remarkable ability to talk and listen at the same time.

"Nice talking to you, Tiko," Guy says as I say good-bye.

Mike's father, for many years a simultaneous translator at the U.N., says that the ability to talk and listen concurrently (which was indispensable for his job), is a talent only certain people have. But again and again I have listened to a flock of parrots all vocalizing at once in the wild. I have the feeling they're listening to one another as well as spouting off, and I think the innate ability to do simultaneous translation may be a generic parrot talent.

Tiko loves music, and mimics it whenever he gets the chance. He sings along with the television, or when Mike and David play guitar together. He is very polite and never starts singing first, although once he gets going, he is fully capable of drowning out a room full of Christmas carolers.

When Mike and Tiko whistle together, Tiko looks quite odd, since he doesn't move his beak (the sound is modulated in the syrinx, a kind of voice box in the lower portion of his windpipe). One day I came upstairs to find Tiko whistling along with the radio. He and Mike were alternating their accompaniment, each waiting patiently for the other to stop before beginning anew. Tiko whistled sotto voce to match the delicate parts, and raised his voice in the louder passages. He was very clear about the distinction between vocals and instrumentals, and he whistled only to instrumentals.

He and Mike have developed quite a repertoire. Tiko rarely whistles with me. Whistling is his special bond with Mike, and he uses it to his advantage. It remains true to this day that whenever he does something to Mike that he knows is naughty (like nip Mike or eat one of his pencils) he flies to the top of the refrigerator and starts to whistle as if to say, "I'm sorry! Can't we be friends?" Mike can't resist. They usually end up doing a long duet, and Mike forgets he was angry.

MIMICRY IN PARROTS is not limited to sounds; some parrots will imitate our gestures. One African Grey I know waves its foot in the air when it says "good night" or "good-bye" to someone who is also waving. Another African Grey imitates the actions of his owner putting on his coat to leave; he uses his wings as arms to enact slipping into each sleeve of the coat. Other parrots learn to nod or shake their heads appropriately, apparently from watching their human companions.

I am inclined to believe that wild parrots are just as much mimics as are captive birds, even though there isn't much science to support this view. Few people study parrot vocalizations in nature; others merely note the squawking and screeching that goes on when parrots fly overhead or feed in the canopy. However, parrots may only mimic other sounds when they are bored or relaxed, and far from human ears. In one night, a recording of two African Greys roosting in Zaire showed that the parrots gave over two hundred different "motifs" or songs, and of these, 23 percent were mimics of nine other bird species and one was of a bat. In view of the amazing mimicry ability African Greys and other parrots demonstrate in captivity, we should devote more time to understanding this capability in the wild.

The ability to mimic sounds may have initially evolved as a method of obtaining prey or avoiding predation. A bird that could mimic the sound of another bird whose eggs or young it wanted to eat could probably entice that bird into responding, giving away its location and potentially the location of its nest.

Similarly, a bird that could mimic its predators could potentially ward them off by suggesting that its territory was already inhabited by a predator, and the newcomer should go hunt somewhere else. This would not have been done with conscious thought, but simply evolved because a bird that could make such sounds would have a better chance of survival, and so a better chance of passing along its mimicry genes to its offspring.

Mimicry, or creating appearances that are deceptive, is not unique to animals. Women emphasize their breasts and men enlarge their shoulders (with shoulder pads in suits) to appear more alluring to the opposite sex or more dangerous to competitors.

I'm often dazzled by Tiko's intelligence. The range of what he understands has expanded dramatically over the years. When I say, "I'm going to work," he flies to the railing by the office and waits for me to put him in his cage. "I'm going out to the garden" provokes flight to the windowsill where he can watch me outside. I tried this over and over, with the same tone of voice and the same inflection: Tiko always knows the difference between the two phrases. If I go downstairs to ride my stationary bike without taking him, Mike is permitted to convey him to me but only if he says, "Come, Tiko, I'll take you to Joanna." Any phrase that includes my name usually results in his willingness to go anywhere with anyone—so it matters little to me at this point if I can't recognize it when he says my name.

7

Watchdog Tiko

TIKO HAD ALWAYS BEEN POSSESSIVE AND PROTECTIVE OF me, but after he began courting me he was especially so. It sometimes seemed that to woo me during the spring and summer and to guard me all year long were the two activities around which his life revolved. The intensity of his connection to me had become almost mind-boggling at times. I suppose dog owners feel the same way about their pets. But dogs don't live sixty or seventy years and form monogamous pair bonds for most of that time. Dogs don't elaborately court their owners. My relationship with Tiko kept deepening, and I began to have some insight into the fierce and tender nature of the intimacy that parrot couples in the wild must share.

Tiko never tired of looking out the office window and warning me against intruders: children in the pool next door, a dog bathing in our frog pond, a deer pruning my tomatoes. Tiko was deathly afraid of the five-foot-long albino Pine Snake I used to keep in the room where I ride my exercise bike. He never took his eyes from it when it slithered about its cage. He called sharply whenever the snake started to move, as if to warn me of impending danger. Only in the winter, when the snake was hibernating, did Tiko relax. Finally, in deference to Tiko's anxieties, I moved the snake to my office at Rutgers.

Tiko's warning calls are distinctive, and they are clearly meant to alert me and Mike, his flock, to danger. If Tiko doesn't think we're in the house, he won't call. Tiko's vigilance, as this behavior is called by biologists, is part of his genetic makeup—as it is for all parrots. Tropical rain forests and dry grain fields are dangerous places, and the flock has developed a sophisticated system of signals to cope with threats.

I was so taken by Tiko's protective attitude toward me that it spurred me to investigate vigilance behavior in a wide range of animals. What began as a small portion of my research quickly grew into a cottage industry that Mike and I shared, coauthoring papers and looking at vigilance behavior all over the world.

I went to Australia in 1996 to study vigilance in the Sulphur-crested Cockatoo, one of the most exotic and spectacular of parrots. The Sulphur is large, with plumage the color and texture of white billowy clouds, the kind of clouds you see from above looking down out of an airplane window. It has a fanciful, recurved yellow crest that waves gently as it moves its head up and down. It forages on the ground, where it's vulnerable to predators—foxes, dogs, and birds of prey, which swoop down from the sky.

We usually see cockatoos as single individuals in cages, so I was totally unprepared for our first encounter in the wild—a flock of forty-eight birds foraging on the ground a hundred miles into the interior from Sydney. The cockatoos were in abandoned farm fields—a flat, windblown, dry country of weeds and grass seed. The brilliance of the birds stood in strong contrast to the desolate brown landscape. They strutted along through the weeds, using their bills to strip the seeds from the long stems that whispered in the hot wind.

At any small social interaction, the cockatoos' crests went bobbing upward, each feather splayed. Many birds have crests (Bluejays, for example) but we almost never see them prominently raised. But the cockatoos were highly sensitive, just like Tiko. God forbid one cockatoo should inadvertently cross the invisible line into another's personal space. The offended bird reacted instantly, sending its crest up like a porcupine raising its quills, after squawking a warning to the trespasser.

Such intrusions could happen innocently enough. The grass was tall, and the birds were intent on foraging. Often the offending bird was oblivious. But sometimes the intrusion was not so innocent. A cockatoo would hear its mate chomping on a particularly fertile patch of seed, sidle over, and covertly begin to whittle away at the prize grass. The bird who had first claimed the patch would call softly, then squawk loudly and, within seconds, lunge at its offending mate—who would move quickly away.

Aside from studying vigilance, I was also in Australia to collect feathers to compare their heavy-metal levels to feathers found in more pristine areas in the highlands of New Guinea, where metal levels are low. I had to get special permission to collect Sulphur feathers because the species is covered by the CITES convention, which protects endangered birds. It was easy to find feathers. When one pair of cockatoos began to preen, suddenly all the pairs started preening. Ethologists call this "social facilitation." Gulls exhibit this trait during the breeding season. When one pair begins to copulate, it immediately sets the others off. Pair after pair assume the position until the scene looks like a Roman orgy. In the cockatoos, the social facilitation of preening leads to an abundance of feathers on the ground wherever the flock stops.

Mike and I loved the outback. It seemed to stretch on forever. The landscape had the primeval feeling of parts of East Africa, and the emptiness of the pampas. It was free from the fetters of civilization, and we returned to Sydney refreshed.

In Sydney, our roll with the cockatoos continued. We found hundreds of them in a green park outside the city! It was thrilling that these birds, which had long been persecuted and captured for the pet trade, were doing so splendidly well, wandering around as common as pigeons—reveled in rather than reviled. They fed in dense flocks, some of the birds facing outward to provide early warning should a predator approach. I inched forward to photograph them feeding. Suddenly, one male cockatoo ran toward me until he was between me and his mate (male cockatoos are slightly larger and their eyes are dark brown, less reddish than the females'). He stopped, glanced her way, spread his crest, and then ran full tilt at me, wings outstretched. This was one of Tiko's postures with Mike, its message clear: "Get away from my mate!"

I watched, delighted and intrigued, as the pure white birds

moved in and out of the gray-green grasses, their yellow crests bobbing over the tops of the vegetation. The birds averaged fifteen inches, and the grass they foraged in was sometimes over their heads, which cut their visibility and made it all the more important to have a good system for vigilance.

Watching cockatoos forage, it was clear to me that they used their fluorescent yellow crest in their vigilance behavior. Birds foraging toward the flock's center watched the sentries stationed on the perimeter for some signal of danger—the extension of a fluorescent feather flashing brilliantly, like a mirror catching the sun.

The raising of their crests, while dramatic to our eyes, was infinitely more so to theirs. Under ultraviolet light their yellow feathers fluoresce brilliantly, lighting up like torches as the crest is raised and lowered gently. I have seen this happening in a lab and it's an amazing sight. Many birds see in this ultraviolet range, although, oddly enough, scientists do not know if parrots do. I suspect that they must, constantly dazzling one another with their plumage. In cockatoos, what appears to us as a very subtle swaying of a pale yellow crest is a bursting flare that signals danger, a warning flag to its male competitors, and a beacon of overwhelming beauty to its mate.

One instance of vigilance was particularly dramatic. I was taking data on what I thought was a small group of birds in a quiet section of the park. Mike, who had come along for the ride but had become bitten by the vigilance bug and had been suckered into helping me collect data, first noticed a dog ambling up the road toward the cockatoos. When the dog caught sight of the birds, it veered excitedly toward them, causing the three birds foraging close to the road to take flight. Suddenly, with a tremendous whoosh, a couple hundred birds burst from the grass into the blue sky, streaming from places we'd thought contained no more than waving grass. The white was almost blinding, and the flock let out a tremendous cacophony of calls, swirling wildly through the air.

It was a breathtaking display, and Mike and I nearly lost our balance in the face of its power and majesty. The poor dog, completely overcome, ran off, its tail between its legs. The flock waited until it was long gone and then settled back down into the grass, most of the birds disappearing from sight.

TIKO'S DEGREE OF VIGILANCE may have been exaggerated from what it would have been in the wild, where vigilance directly relates to survival. If an animal's attention wanders, it gets eaten. But vigilance comes at a cost: a vigilant animal can't court or forage. Because we provided Tiko with a never-ending smorgasbord of delicacies, there was no cost to his vigilance. He was therefore constantly on guard, a tireless watchdog.

When I teach the concept of vigilance to my students, they often confuse it with territoriality. This is not surprising, since the two behaviors are often linked. Vigilance refers to keeping a lookout—for predators, competitors, potential mates. Territoriality refers to defending a space for breeding, feeding, or rearing young. One must be vigilant when defending a territory, but it's a vigilance directly related to maintaining your space. Vigilance need not have anything to do with territory. Tiko was being vigilant when he looked out the window to warn me of danger, and territorial when he ran Mike out of his room.

There has been much more science on territoriality than on vigilance. Territoriality was first observed in bird life at the beginning of the twentieth century by Eliot Howard, author of *Territory in Bird Life,* which was published in 1920 and was the first real, detailed description of territoriality. Educated at Eton and Mason's College, Howard, a steel-master by trade and director of Stewarts and Lloyds steel firm, was a hobbyist. Like many amateurs he contributed immensely to our knowledge of birds. Since birds are diurnal, Howard and others could watch them in the mornings before work.

Concepts of territoriality can be traced back to Aristotle, who noted that where food is insufficient for more birds than two, ravens are only found in isolated pairs. The swan-masters of late-sixteenth-century England recognized that swans had their own breeding grounds. Thus the thought was there; it just took Howard to formulate it.

Initially, Howard studied the territorial behavior of warblers. He saw that each male isolated itself at the beginning of the breeding season, and exercised dominion over a restricted area of ground (what we now recognize as territory). Howard then provided extensive descriptions of territoriality in many different species and showed the generality of the phenomena among very different species of birds, such as crows, shrikes, warblers, blackbirds, owls, hawks, shorebirds, and doves. As with so many scientific ideas, it is often the sheer volume of examples that is persuasive. He continued to publish on the topic until the 1940s.

Following Howard, Ernst Mayr, who is still going strong at Harvard at nearly one hundred years old, was one of the first to make an analytical classification of the types of territories (1935): mating, the feeding of young, colonial species versus solitary species. In 1941, Margaret Morse Nice produced a modification of Mayr's classification, adding winter and roosting territories. What was becoming clear is that birds have different kinds of territories both during and after the breeding season.

Konrad Lorenz incorporated territorial concepts into an overall view of the social life of birds, particularly Jackdaws. Lorenz, and later Niko Tinbergen (two of only three scientists ever to win the Nobel Prize for work on animal behavior—fancy that!), explored the functions of territoriality—linking territoriality with survival and reproductive success. I once had the opportunity to talk with Tinbergen in his Oxford office. It was a thrilling experience. His genius for conducting experiments on behavior without wrenching animals from their natural environment has deeply influenced my work.

In the 1970s, biologists began to study the ways birds defend territory and linked that to their behavior as they guard against predators. Thus the link was made between vigilance and territoriality. In order to acquire and defend a territory, a bird has to watch for intruders and judge whether the intruder is worth responding to. But vigilance is much more than that; it is looking for space, mates, competitors, nest sites, nest material, food, and predators. In fact, being aware of our surroundings is vigilance, and without it birds would lose their mates and territories, go hungry, and fall prey.

Early studies of vigilance by Ronald Pulliam in 1973 showed that animals that foraged in groups had higher probability of detecting predators than those not in groups. For the next fifteen years, a rash of papers showed that as group size increased, time devoted to vigilance decreased. William Hamilton then posed the selfish herd concept—you have less chance of being taken by a predator if you are in a group. The lion takes only one animal at a time, and hopefully it won't be you.

Mike's and my contribution to this field of inquiry was to more broadly apply the concept of vigilance. We studied vigilance in Ostriches in Kenya, finding that an increase in group size results in a decrease in each animal's vigilance. But we also found that males devoted more time to vigilance, and we proposed that they were looking for male competitors—their vigilance was focused on competition for mates, not just predator protection. We also found that while males spent more time in vigilant behavior during the early phases of the breeding cycle (when they have to worry about finding females), female wildebeests and impalas increase their vigilance time when they have vulnerable young.

The field has exploded, with many studies examining the different factors that affect vigilance, such as age, sex, cover, distance to cover, and so on. Mike and I helped create that explosion, arguing, I think convincingly, that vigilance is a much more generalized behavior than territoriality, which has to do with defending space or defending one's mate during the breeding season. Vigilance occurs year-round; it is an integral part of day-to-day behavior.

It wasn't much of a leap to apply Tiko's behavior to vigilance in other animals and man. We are constantly vigilant—about where our food and shelter will come from, our job security, potential dangers like approaching cars, people, possible muggers, or someone making eyes at our mate. In fact, we're vigilant both subliminally and consciously just about all the time. Vigilance is one of the characteristics of our awareness of the world around us, and I've often thought that a drop in vigilance is a symptom of depression: the depressive is dulled to what's going on around him. But I can also imagine transcendental states where vigilance fades, replaced by awareness that is pervasive, undefended, no longer moored in what is perhaps the crux of our sense of self.

TIKO WAS EVER VIGILANT in defending me, his territory, and himself—and the territory he considered his own gradually expanded from his feeding perches to his room and nest sites to my exercise room and, finally, to all he surveyed from the windows of our house. He was particularly possessive about the room that housed his cage. When we'd begun to renovate our office, we'd moved him into Debbie's room to spare him the headaches of construction. It had become my slide-projection, sewing, and dressing room when Debbie had headed off to graduate school—that is, until Tiko took it over.

He graciously allowed me to enter to dress each morning, a ritual he appreciated because while I was there he could show me his nesting hole under the dresser, crooning softly all the time. He'd run under it and peek out, head nearly touching the rug, making sure I was still giving him my full attention. If I tarried too long deciding what to wear, Tiko would come over, stand on the floor on one foot, wrap his four toes around my big toe, and preen himself. It was as if we were holding hands.

Mike and I managed to work around most of Tiko's territorial defenses, but when he appropriated the refrigerator we had a real problem. The refrigerator top, a favorite perch, was the highest point in the kitchen. From there Tiko was lord of all he surveyed. He made sure the cooking, serving, and cleaning up were to his liking. But because he perched on it he began to consider the refrigerator his territory and lunged at anyone except me who tried to open its door.

I tried, with limited success, to cajole him. Berating him would have put his back up. The way to get him to listen is to soothe him, lull him. "Tiko, sweetheart," I said, "you have to let other people into the refrigerator. I can't do this all myself. It doesn't hurt you, and we need to get dinner on the table."

This little speech, delivered in dulcet tones, usually calmed him. His receptive vocabulary is such that he understood exactly what it was that I was saying, smoothed his feathers, and stopped lunging and flashing his eyes. With great dignity and deliberation he straightened from his pugnacious stance. He radiated magnanimity; but, alas, it was short-lived. Five minutes later he was back at it, crouched down, talons grasping the refrigerator door's hinge, and Mike reaching out, arm fully extended, keeping his body as far away from Tiko's beak as possible, trying to be quick and agile, reaching into the box as though there were a live rattlesnake inside, going for the pitcher of juice or the jam or some innocuous item that Tiko wouldn't touch with a ten-foot pole, and the parrot making these silent and deadly lunges, which are very effective and deliberate. I could see that he was giving Mike time to move away, that he didn't really want to hurt him. Mike, however, was not amused.

It's a royal pain and I wish that I could report to you that the bird has outgrown this behavior, and that I am never a player in these shenanigans. Such, unfortunately, is not the case. It happens like this: Tiko knows I'm getting a particular food in the refrigerator that he likes, and that I'm not going to give him any. The bird is a fiend for cheese, for example, which would clog his arteries, and I ration it.

"No, Tiko," I say. "You know you can't have any of this cheese. We don't want you to have high cholesterol and get sick."

He becomes testy, peevishly pecking at the strip of rubber insulation around the refrigerator door.

"Tiko, please don't do that. You're hurting the door. It won't keep our food cold."

He takes umbrage at these no's and lunges at me.

We have had long, involved discussions about the refrigerator, Tiko and I—not that they have done much good. These altercations are ongoing, an unresolved border dispute that if we lived that long would drag on for centuries. Talking to Tiko about this usually doesn't accomplish much. In the short term he listens. But soon, he's up to his old tricks. We have ended up working around him, letting him sit atop the fridge while we make dinner. If we need something, I open its door. Guests are duly warned. And for Mike, although he's learned to be quick and keep out of Tiko's reach, the food in his own refrigerator is sometimes off-limits.

OVER THE YEARS, Tiko's territorial behavior has become a bit problematic in the bedroom. When Mike and I watch television at night, Tiko insists on standing between us. He allows me free movement, but he squawks angrily if Mike presumes to move even a hair closer to me. I actually very seldom watch television. Most likely, I will be half watching it, reading while Mike and Tiko watch the news. They're also fans of *Friends* and *Cheers* reruns, shows that, for me, long ago lost their charm. Along with Chinese food and whistling, television is an indulgence shared by the boys. Tiko watches people parade across the screen, sings along with the commercials, and calls with gusto should he be lucky enough to encounter a parrot on the screen. Those are wonderful, rare moments and provide high excitement for all of us. Since Tiko's taken to snoozing all day while we're at the office, at eleven P.M., as we're winding down and looking forward to some quiet quality time together, he's wide awake and hypervigilant.

The bird does not miss a trick. He sits on the pillow above my right hand. Mike is to my left. There is an expanse of bed between us. Handholding, or perhaps a hand placed casually on my shoulder, is permissible. But should Mike have the audacity to inch closer to me or, worse yet, caress my face or put both arms around me or, heaven forbid, kiss me, Tiko will shoot across the pillow to peck Mike's head. I, on the other hand, can touch Mike whenever and wherever I want. My touch does not arouse Tiko's ire. But other ways in which I interact with Mike do.

Tiko is focused on my eyes. In bed I am allowed, by the parrot who owns me, brief covert glances at the man I married. Should I gaze upon my husband for any more than a minute, Tiko marches across the pillow toward Mike's head. Likewise, I can talk to Mike, but a certain affectionate tone provokes an immediate attack—on Mike, of course, not me, although I am the perpetrator of the crime. Sexual intimations in my voice—a melting sigh, a soft *ummm*, a slight panting or tightness in the chest—send Tiko into a fury. He crosses the coverlet to duke it out with Mike, *mano a mano*. Or, should I say, beak to hand. Mike has to leave the room, and it takes quite a while for me to calm the bird down, putting him to bed in his cage and talking to him in the sweetest, most reassuring tones, telling him over and over how much I love him.

DURING THE DAY, while I work on my computer, Tiko stands behind me, perched by the window. Sometimes he sleeps, but mostly he peers out at the backyard and the patch of sky above the low forest of Black Locust, Silver Maple, oak, and ornamental cherry that stretches southward from the house for a mile or so. Long before I spot anything in the sky, Tiko detects an incoming threat while the hawk is still a dot in the sky. He gives his frantic hawk warning call, fluttering from his perch, scattering papers in his wake, waddling as fast as his stubby legs can carry him under Mike's desk, where he hides behind a barricade of stacked boxes.

Over the years, I have come to distinguish Tiko's hawk warning call from his cat warning call. His tone also indicates whether the hawk is perched on a branch or in flight. It's difficult to describe exactly how these calls differ: there are subtle variations in tone, intensity, and volume. Some calls, the one for a hawk, for instance, are repeated rapidly; others aren't.

Tiko's genetic memory of predators involves jaguars and snakes as well as hawks. Since parrots are most often in the canopy, jaguars are hard-pressed to take them. Cats, of course, can climb. But I've yet to see one that could fly. The parrots are much more vulnerable to the cats if they venture down toward the jungle floor. They might also be taken at night by Tayras or Margays. Tayras are mustelids (a family including minks and weasels) that feed in the trees on birds as large as chickens. Margays are endangered spotted cats, agile climbers that eat monkeys, rodents, birds, and lizards.

Snakes, both venomous and constrictor, wrap themselves around a tree branch and lie in wait for birds of all types. The snakes are almost impossibly patient and perfectly camouflaged; they can stay absolutely still for hours, perhaps even days, at a stretch. Should a hapless parrot land within striking distance, the snake has a good shot at it. Constrictors will even pursue a bird through the canopy for a short distance.

But these incidents are rare. The real danger to Red-lored Amazons are raptors: Collared Forest-falcons, and Gray-headed, Bicolored, Great Black, and Bay-winged Hawks. Hawk eagles glide, circling so far up we often can't see them with the naked eye, positioning themselves so they are lost in blinding sunlight.

It's rare that a mature parrot will get caught by a hawk. But a young bird may be slow to respond to a warning call, or will venture too far from the shelter of the trees. The hawk will dive, wings folded into its body, plummeting down at an incredible speed. The hawk's aim is nothing short of miraculous, diving as one does from a great height with only minor corrections to hit such a small target. The parrot will often be killed on impact, or stunned. The hawk makes a tight loop and retrieves the dead or dying bird as it drops. If the hawk misses on the first pass, it will pursue the parrot through the air in a bobbing, lurching aerial ballet. The parrot will swoop toward the canopy. In the dense girders of vines and branches, the parrot's short-winged maneuverability gives it an edge over the long-winged power of the hawks. But sometimes even this advantage is not enough.

WHEN TIKO GAVE his hawk call, Mike and I would invariably spot a Red-tailed, Sharp-shinned, or Cooper's Hawk flying overhead or perched in a nearby tree. Tiko's response was so consistent that there was no question that he recognized hawkdom. To our amazement, he didn't panic when a Herring Gull, crow, or Canada Goose flew overhead, species that Tinbergen found confused some birds. Not even when he spied a Turkey Vulture, a raptor with a hawklike shape, would he take cover. Tiko knew a hawk when he saw one.

He would emerge from under the desk only if I crooned, "It's all right, Tiko, the hawk has gone," or after hiding for fifteen minutes, a long time for a creature who wants to spend all his time within sight of his flock-mates. No amount of coaxing on Mike's part could convince Tiko to emerge before he felt ready. He only dove for the desk if the hawk was coming toward the window—it was an instinctual response, the same way we blink when something moves quickly toward our face. If a hawk was just flying around outside, he'd call to warn me of the danger, but he didn't feel compelled to take cover. He'd call and call, jabbering in an anxious monologue, until I said, "It's okay, I see it." Only then would he fall silent, watching the raptor through the window with a wary expression, clearly on guard until it was long gone.

8

Our Knight in Shining Feathers

TIKO AS WATCHDOG IS OFTEN AMUSING AND OCCASION-ally annoying, but it once saved a life. And once it almost cost one. After Tiko had been with us about ten years, one warm spring day Mike found a wounded Belted Kingfisher below his office window. This happens often enough; birds mistake the reflection of sky and clouds in glass windows for open space. They hit the glass with a loud thud, crash to the ground, and lie there, stunned or dying. If they're only stunned, in the hour or two it takes them to recuperate they're sitting ducks for cats and other predators that happen by. Early on in our house, Tiko tried to walk through a window. He never did it again, but small birds, it seems, are not as sharp.

The only thing to do if you've found such a bird is to move it to a protected place; if it doesn't die immediately, it will usually recover in a couple of hours. Mike brought the kingfisher home in a box, intending to release it when it was strong enough to fly. It was a dark blue chunky bird, a little smaller than Tiko, with a long, massive black bill. Kingfishers usually live near rivers or streams, digging nest burrows in a mud or sand bank. Most migrate south for the winter, some as far as Florida, although a few remain up north, near us. Belted Kingfishers have a dark band striped across their white breasts, giving them their name. Their strong heads and bills are perfectly adapted to the way in which they make their living, diving for fish. Our kingfisher was still quite weak, and, although it could stand, it wasn't moving about. It needed rest. We left the box in the downstairs foyer outside the room with my exercise bike. Later that evening, I went to ride. As is my custom, I quickly became engrossed in a murder mystery. I pumped away on the bike, the belt around the front wheel making a hypnotic whirring sound. Breath came in a deep steady stream in and out of my lungs. Thumping sounds stirred the darkness as a husband was stabbed and a young wife fled from an attacker. She tripped on the front steps, and then ran wildly through the woods, her hair catching in the dark branches, her feet stumbling over the broken ground. Don't ask me why I'm such a sucker for these books. They temporarily mask the boredom of riding a bike indoors. I became so caught up that it took me a minute or two to register that the thumping from the kingfisher's box in the foyer wasn't part of the story.

All at once I remembered the injured bird. My first thought was for Tiko. The kingfisher's bill is built for pressure and strength; Tiko would be in trouble if the kingfisher attacked him. I ran to the foyer to find Tiko standing on the edge of the carton, vigorously striking the cowering kingfisher on the head. The thumping I'd heard was the bill of the kingfisher knocking the side of the box as it cringed in the corner, frantically trying to escape Tiko's beak. The kingfisher had no business in Tiko's house, in his territory.

We rescued the kingfisher, and moved the box to a closed room. I was relieved that Tiko hadn't given it a heart attack. Tiko posted himself by the closed door of the room where the kingfisher was confined to make sure the bird didn't escape.

The next afternoon, we took the kingfisher in its box out to the backyard. It was spring—the ground was awakening from a particularly snowy winter. The daffodils were blooming, the red tulips just beginning to open. The leaves on the Black Locust were still plump brown buds. But the sun was warm, bathing the yard in the promise of summer. Tiko flew down to the bicycle room so he could watch us through the garden window. Mike opened the box, lifted out the kingfisher, and opened his hand. For a minute the kingfisher looked around, assessed its surroundings; then it flew in a straight line toward the trees beyond our frog pond.

We walked back into the house, and, with the intruder gone, Tiko flew to my shoulder for a ride back to our office. For years a kingfisher came to our pond to feed on the small goldfish, and I imagined that this was the bird Mike had saved from the jaws of a cat or dog.

Tiko was obviously jealous of the kingfisher, and jealousy and territoriality in both animals and humans are intimately linked. Tiko doesn't want me to pay attention to another animal (and that includes my husband), an instinctual response that is part of "pair-bond maintenance"; this generally occurs in birds during a female's fertile periods, to protect against insemination of sperm into the female by males other than the female's mate. The same thing happens in primates. The dominant male spends an enormous amount of time consorting with females that are in heat, asserting his bond and keeping away would-be suitors.

Since human beings can copulate at any time, the jealous, territorial response is generalized. This also happens in some birds, especially where the pair bond is maintained throughout the year. It is strongest during courtship, mating, and egg-laying. But the male is also protective and territorial around the female during egg incubation; if the eggs are lost the female will begin her cycle again, jeopardizing the male's paternity.

Tiko's jealous, possessive behavior continued throughout the year, even though it was strongest in spring. There is a biological reason for this in human beings as well as birds. If the pair bond is strong and solid, reproduction is easier when the time is ripe, and the offspring of a stable pair have a better chance to survive and prosper. It's interesting that sexual defense behavior, which may spawn jealousy, is largely a male trait in the animal world. Males have no way of ensuring that they are the father of their mate's offspring unless they guard their females night and day. Female aggression comes into play in birds in defending food and space for their eggs and young. A female will also guard against the intrusion of other females to prevent a newcomer from trying to coax away her mate or usurp space for a nest.

EVEN A HAPPILY PAIRED PARROT needs friends, and until the kingfisher incident I'd often thought of getting Tiko a companion. Tiko was not atypical. Parrots bonded to humans often become hostile when another bird enters their territory. If two young birds grow up together, there is a good chance they'll become close companions—but trying to make this happen after the juvenile stage is a roll of the dice. Often the two birds will end up wanting to kill each other, simultaneously demanding the attention of the human companions and making life miserable for everyone involved.

Why would a parrot choose a human mate over one of its own kind? This type of behavior does have a parallel in the wild. Parrots have been known to select a mate of the same sex and not show any interest in a bird that is more reproductively appropriate. They've also been known to select a mate of a different species. It's sometimes hard to know why this occurs. Early on, perhaps, a parrot ended up with a flock of a different species, and came to recognize it as its own. Such things happen most often in captivity, where the choice of mates is limited, but it can also happen in the wild. On a recent trip to Nebraska, Mike and I saw a European Crane mated to a Sandhill Crane. The same pair had been around the year before. I've seen the same kind of pairing happen in gulls.

Even though Tiko does not have a live bird to keep him company, over the years he has cultivated a circle of friends. During the harrowing months when Rutgers was deciding whether or not to promote me to full professor, to distract myself and pass the time I carved a flock of wooden owls. I placed them in the living room, around the stone flanges of the fireplace and on its mantle. Perhaps because they are so still and silent, they do not threaten him in the same way the kingfisher did, and Tiko often sits with these wooden creatures. He bends his head down and rubs the back of his neck against their wooden beaks. He reposes among them, eyes half closed, enjoying their silent companionship, and I am always both amused and touched that he has adopted this flock as his own. He is happy to hang out with them for hours at a time if I'm close by. But it goes without saying that he abandons them without a backward glance should I leave the room.

Since Tiko would not allow another pet in the house, I settled on an outdoor pet, a female Rhode Island Red Chicken named Hester. One day, when I was visiting my older brother Melvin, I had clucked over his beautiful fowls and confessed that I'd always wanted a pet chicken. "Why not take one of mine?" he said, and the deed was done. He put Hester, as I dubbed her, in a brown paper bag, and I took her back to Somerset.

Hester loved it in our backyard. Her large cage was cozy, covered with a rug and plastic to keep out the cold. She could go in and out at will through its open door, and she partook freely of the copious food we put out for the wild birds. She spent her days scratching under the bushes for worms and insects, and at the end of each busy day, she'd walk to the base of the table where her cage was, take aim, and flap awkwardly up to the tabletop. She'd bustle into her cage, settle on her nest of straw, and snuggle down for the night. She grew quite fond of the crows, starlings, Bluejays, and squirrels that shared our yard and foraged with her, and she watched them for signs of danger. She never looked skyward herself; they were her alarm system.

She was devoted to us, following us around the yard, running to keep up, stopping only a few steps behind us. If we gardened in one place, she'd scratch for grubs, insects, and earthworms at our feet. When I worked in the raised flower beds, she'd flap up to search for worms there, anxious to be near me. She sometimes bordered on being underfoot, but she was adorable nonetheless.

She knew her name. When I'd call, "Hester," she'd come racing across the yard, especially after we started feeding her crickets. We discovered her cricket craving by chance. We fed crickets to the frogs in our pond to provide them with extra energy in the late fall, just before they went into hibernation. Hester started coming to the pond to snatch up the crickets before the Green Frogs could get to them. She'd even lean over the bank to grab them from the surface of a lily pad. The cold weather came early the first year we had Hester. The frogs went into hibernation, drifting to the pond bottom, burrowing into the mud, leaving us with nearly five hundred crickets. Hester was delighted and she polished them off! She began to eye us critically when none appeared, jumping two feet in the air to peer into our hands, calling insistently.

From his window perch, Tiko would scrutinize these goings-on. When I was outside with Hester, he fussed and called—an insistent contact call that said, "Come back into the house this instant!" plain as day. Hester drove him to the brink of madness. He'd be waiting for me, having flown downstairs lickety-split as soon as he'd deduced from my movements that I was coming back inside. He'd land on my shoulder and snap peevishly at me before flying back upstairs to brood and sulk, expecting me to follow. If I didn't, he'd fly back to my shoulder and remain there, clinging tightly. The intensity of his response bordered on hysteria during his breeding season.

Tiko took to moodily watching Hester, even when I wasn't outside with her. Who knows what was going through his parrot brain? He followed her progress around the backyard as she scratched and clucked. She was oblivious. It never crossed her mind that she was being observed. Did Tiko feel disdain for this creature that dined on worms? I would have guessed he wished her dead, gone to roost with the great chicken in the sky. But events were to prove me wrong.

I still can't say I fully understand what happened one chilly early spring day, about six months after Hester's advent into our lives. I was working on my computer when Tiko gave a loud squawk and ran, hunched over, along his perch toward the window. "Mike," I called, "there's something outside. Tiko's warning us."

Tiko's calls are our wildlife beacon—without them, we'd often remain at our desks, oblivious to the creatures passing through our backyard. It clearly wasn't a hawk—Tiko didn't seem sufficiently panicked. We rushed to the window. I didn't see anything. Suddenly Mike cried, "Hester!" and bolted downstairs. Then I saw—a large dog was mauling Hester! He had her pinned down and was gnawing at her.

Mike dashed into the yard as I pounded on the window. The dog fled and I ran downstairs, making sure, even in that awful moment, to shut the office door so Tiko wouldn't slip outside in the commotion.

Hester hobbled toward us, listing to one side. I scooped her into my arms. But for Tiko's warning, she would have been chopped liver. Feathers drifted in all directions as she huddled against me, whimpering softly, drooping her head. She didn't usually want to be held tightly, preferring to perch instead on my arm or lap. This time, however, she snuggled deeper into my body. I rocked her gently. "You'll be all right, Hester," I whispered. "Hang in there." But the feathers kept coming off, and I could feel her small heart racing, as though it was going to burst. Her body shook uncontrollably.

As I held Hester, I wondered if Tiko had understood she was in danger. Had he participated intentionally in her rescue? His reaction had been different than his typical response to a dog wandering through the yard—then his calls stopped when I said, "It's okay, Tiko." This time, though, he'd kept calling, ignoring me. He'd run back and forth, tremendously upset. Had Hester become part of his extended flock?

I wanted to see if Hester could stand, so I placed her on the table just inside her cage. I watched in horror as she limped toward me and then collapsed.

"The dog broke her leg!" I said to Mike through clenched teeth. I felt like screaming.

Mike picked up Hester and gently traced the bones in her leg with his physician's hands. His fingers lingered on each of her joints. "I think it's just a sprain," he finally said, much to my relief.

I carried Hester inside, walking through the house and crooning to her softly. A trail of red-tinged feathers drifted in our wake, and we quickly discovered why. Gently pushing aside her wing, we found a gaping hole. The feathers had been ripped out all around the wound. I set her down, but she could no longer stand upright, and toppled over. Mike dashed upstairs for antibiotic cream.

We smeared the cream over the wound, held her, and then put her in a small box with soft towels. We covered her, talking softly, trying to lessen her trauma. Whenever an animal is injured, it needs to rest in darkness, quietly, without moving.

It was only then that we registered Tiko's angry calls from inside the closed office door. I made my way hastily upstairs. The hours dragged by. We were both sick with worry. Our little family had been violated. Every hour I left Tiko and Mike in the office, went downstairs, picked Hester up, crooned to her, made sure the antibiotic was still covering the wound, and returned her to the quiet solitude of her box. We offered her water, which she eagerly drank; she ignored the cricket we tried to give her. We checked on her every hour through the night. Birds often lose their voices after traumas, but by midnight she was beginning to answer our greetings with a very soft cluck, although it was hardly audible.

In the morning, she was slightly better, calling more strongly and even standing, though she didn't want to walk about. We hand-fed her, slipping crickets into her opened bill. By late morning she was strong enough to snatch the crickets from my palm. We couldn't leave her in the box all day—she needed food, water, and to move around so she didn't stiffen up. We hit upon housing her in the downstairs bathroom.

We outfitted the room with food and water and lined the floor with newspaper, leaving a stack on the countertop. We went to school, taught, and rushed home to find Hester contentedly sitting in the sink. In our absence, she'd hopped on the john and then up to the countertop, pulled the newspaper into the sink, shredded it, and shifted it about to make a comfortable nest. One pale brown egg sat in the middle of this pile of confetti.

I was ecstatic that she was doing so well, and proud of her fast recovery. I cooed to her, showering her with tenderness and affection. Suddenly, Tiko careened onto my shoulder and began ferociously pecking my hair. Sweet-talking another bird—and a chicken at that! How could I? I left Hester to Mike and carried Tiko upstairs. Fifteen minutes of allopreening and he was back to his old self. But after that incident, where I clearly proved myself to be a wanton flirt, he wouldn't let me out of his sight.

He insisted on coming downstairs with me to make sure I was riding the bicycle and not talking to Hester. In the past I'd often said, "Tiko, I'm going to ride the bike. Do you want to come?" I'd offer him my hand, and he'd sometimes bow his head, indicating that he was in no mood to move. He would peck at me if I didn't leave him alone. He'd wait upstairs about ten minutes and then, when he was good and ready, either come down to join me on his own or call to Mike, whom he'd trained to offer him shuttle service. Tiko would hop on Mike's wrist and Mike would convey him to his destination. But was the parrot grateful for the ride? Not on your life! The instant Mike placed him on the bookshelf across from the exercise bike, Tiko lunged at him. Mike had (and has) no business in my exercise room, except as Tiko's chauffeur. But when Tiko knew Hester was in the house, the second I left the office he was on my heels—even when I told him I was just going to the bathroom. I had to be wily to sneak in visits to my convalescing chick. I'd distract Tiko with pinyon nuts and then surreptitiously creep downstairs.

We decided to keep Hester in the house until she was completely healed. This gave us time to fence in the yard, preventing any further accidents. Friends pointed out the idiocy of paying a thousand dollars to fence a yard for a chicken—but Hester was one of the family.

As the days passed, Hester seemed to grow bored with the bathroom. So one afternoon I decided to let her walk around a bit. That was when Tiko had finally had enough. Was the chicken now being given full run of his house? He swooped into the downstairs foyer, landed on the freezer we keep there, glanced briefly at Hester, and glared at me. He hunched down, swayed from side to side to get a good visual fix, extended his wings, and stalked toward the petrified chicken. She scooted over to me, calling softly. Before I realized what was happening, Tiko had landed on her back and was savagely pecking at her head—despite the fact that Hester was over twice his size. She ran to throw him off, flying up to Mike's workbench, scattering paper, seeds, and tools, frantically scrabbling for a safe place to land. Tiko homed in on her like a heat-seeking missile. He grabbed her back with his talons and lunged at her head with his beak. She squawked wildly, but he was silent, deadly, intent. The two birds swirled around the floor as I tried to separate them. Mike appeared and reached for Hester. He was barefoot and Tiko furiously pecked his toes. When I approached Tiko to try to pick him up he made it very clear, with his exaggerated lunge and hostile, rasping call, that he was willing to take my finger off. While I distracted Tiko by talking to him and using my body to shield the chicken from his view, Mike grabbed Hester and locked her in the bathroom. With obvious finality, Tiko flew from the room to his upstairs perch, where he sulked for nearly two hours. The indignities we expected him to endure were simply unbearable. I coddled him and talked to him in the sweetest tones. Finally, he came over, climbed up on my shoulder, and preened my hair, calling softly. Was he apologizing to me or forgiving my transgression?

From then on I'd sit with Tiko upstairs, feed him, preen him, talk to him, and then explain, "I have to go downstairs to feed Hester. You just have to cope." I'd shut the office door behind me. Normally, Tiko would have made a huge fuss if he got shut in a room, screaming at the top of his lungs. But perhaps because I explained what I was doing, he was quiet until I returned, and then he seemed to ignore me with only a touch of petulance at the fact that I was carrying on with another bird.

SUMMER FINALLY CAME, the yard was fenced, and Hester was once again a free-range chicken. Tiko watched her from his window perch as she grubbed through our flower beds. He continued to respond to her interactions with me. If I was sitting on our backyard swing and Hester came over to solicit crickets, Tiko seemed relatively untroubled. If I had no crickets and Hester jumped up onto my knee, that was too much. Tiko gave a long, angry contact call that grew to a loud scream, which he repeated until I put her down. But there seemed to be a softening and even a curiosity in his attitude toward her. When I rode my bicycle, instead of focusing on me (his habitual pose), I'd see him looking out the window, watching her. It was my turn to feel slight pangs of jealousy. He'd stare at her as if he was demented, smitten, or both. She took to flying to the top of the compressor unit of our central air conditioner, where she would perch. She and Tiko would spend long hours looking at each other through the pane of glass, occasionally exchanging soft calls. Did she know that he had saved her life—that he was her knight in shining feathers? Even with the odd rapport they seemed to have developed, I still didn't dare take Hester inside. Tiko's territorial response was simply too strong. I knew all too well that the besotted paramour could turn instantly into Hannibal Lecter.

Hester's demise wrenched me. One dark night when I was away and Tiko was not there to protect or warn her, she was captured by a fox, which fed her to its own offspring that lived in a den in the woods behind our house. We gave her feathers a burial under our purple Butterfly Bush. I took solace in the golden-red color of the young foxes that cavorted in the grass that summer. They were the same color as Hester.

9

In Sickness and in Health

IT WAS PARTIALLY TIKO'S INFLUENCE THAT LED MY RE-search away from pure science into issues that directly affect the health of both human beings and animals. Tiko made me see that we are all in this together. Our fate is intimately connected to the fate of wild creatures with which we are entwined in the web of life that sustains us all.

So it was that I have found myself in recent years going more and more to Washington for closed-door meetings in the staid, wood-paneled rooms of the National Academy of Sciences. The academy is located right across the street from the State Department. I gather with other scientists to debate hot-button issues and write reports for the Environmental Protection Agency, the U.S. Fish and Wildlife Service, the Departments of Energy and the Interior, and other governmental agencies. These reports often go to

Congress and the President, and influence public policy decisions that affect us all.

One such series of meetings led to the regulations that required shrimp fishermen to use turtle excluders on their nets. Sea turtles were being inadvertently snared in the shrimpers' nets, where they drowned. The excluders provide a way for the turtles to escape without any loss of shrimp. Because the excluders were a new technology, shrimpers were wary of them. The academy committee's deliberations provided Congress with the necessary science for writing the excluders into law. Other committees have dealt with the dolphin kills in the world tuna fishery, ungulate overgrazing in Yellowstone National Park, and whether chemicals in the environment act as endocrine disrupters.

My work with the academy began in the mid-1980s, when I became involved with the National Research Council, an immensely influential but little known arm of the National Academy. The council is set up in a hierarchical system of committees, boards, and commissions, whose members serve on a volunteer basis. Being asked to serve is a professional responsibility that mid-career-and-above scientists do for a variety of reasons. There is immense prestige in serving on a high post within the council. An appointment can advance your academic career, and participation on the boards provides an independent validation of your expertise, which can be influential when you go to obtain funding for your own research projects. Although there is no honorarium or compensation for your time, the council does pay travel expenses to attend its meetings. You get to hobnob with colleagues, and lots of cross-pollination of ideas goes on. The committees bring together people in different disciplines, and this broadens your perspective. But the main reason to participate in the council and its activities is that you're able to influence policy on a national level. The council is where the action is.

I broadened my interest in the effects of contaminants on animal behavior as a result of my discussions with scientists on the council's Board of Environmental Studies and Toxicology. In a sense, we were second-generation scientists after Rachel Carson, the author of the vastly influential book *Silent Spring,* which did so much to raise public awareness and focus scientists on the potential danger of introducing man-made chemicals into our air, soil, and water.

I often thought of *Silent Spring* through the mid-1980s and early 1990s as I began to observe mysteriously low rates of reproductive success in some birds in certain breeding colonies. I couldn't account for it on the basis of increased predation, low food supplies, or human disturbance alone, and I began to think, as I talked about these observations with my colleagues, that low-level contaminants might be a culprit.

In the summer of 1993, I set out to do fieldwork on Herring Gulls at Captree State Park on Long Island to investigate this hypothesis. The study, conducted by Mike and me for the National Institute of Environmental Health Sciences, was the culmination of ten years of laboratory research on the effects of low-level lead exposure on the behavioral development of birds. Behavioral toxicology, as this field of study is known, is usually done in the laboratory using rats and mice. Mike and I were the first team to leave the laboratory to look at the effects of lead on birds in the wild.

Lead, mercury, cadmium, and other pollutants spewed into the atmosphere by industry and automobiles are borne on the wind, and are brought to earth by dust or rain. This fallout, which comes mostly from the Northern Hemisphere, finds its way into the most remote corners of our world. Birds ingest lead and mercury by eating fish that have ingested invertebrates, which, in turn, have absorbed metals through their skin. Adélie Penguins in Antarctica have mercury in their feather shafts and barbs. So do Gough Island Wandering and Sooty Albatrosses in the deepest reaches of the stormy southern Atlantic, Sooty Shearwaters living off Peru's southern coast, and the small Sparrow Hawks of northern Finland and Norway.

Though lead has been found in plants and animals in the most remote areas, it's much more heavily concentrated in cities and along roadsides. Leaded gasoline is still used in many countries, and lead-based paints are chipping off walls into the soil and surface water both here and abroad. Well-publicized studies by Herbert Needleman and colleagues from the University of Pittsburgh, begun in the late 1970s, found an average six-point decrease in the IQs of inner-city children in Boston and Philadelphia who were exposed to lead paint on the walls of the buildings in which they lived.

Looking at Needleman's studies, Mike and I began to wonder if lead was altering gull chicks' behavior in ways that affected their survival. In our laboratory at Rutgers we exposed Herring Gull chicks to low lead levels. This disrupted their ability to walk, feed, find shade, and avoid heat stress. The chicks were fifteen days old before they recognized their parents. Normal chicks do so in six or seven days, and for good reason: six-day-old chicks typically begin to wander from their nests. If they wander outside their territory, there's a good chance they'll be cannibalized by their neighbors, so it's critical that they are able to recognize and approach only their parents.

Our plan at Captree was to see if chicks in the wild with lead levels similar to our lab chicks would have similar behavioral problems. We wondered if these problems would be more or less pronounced. And we were also interested in the flip side of the equation. How would parents respond to impaired chicks? Would they reject, coddle, or treat them in the same way as their unimpaired offspring?

In May, I set up shop at Captree, planning to spend ten weeks watching a Herring Gull colony of several hundred birds. Mike came up for a week during the hatching period in late May and measured lead levels in the chicks. He marked the chicks with different-colored leg bands to identify individual birds. I didn't know which chicks had the high lead levels, since being able to objectively observe the behavior of each clutch precluded knowing which chicks were potentially impaired.

After Mike was done with measuring and marking, he returned to Somerset. While he had been with me at Captree, Tiko had been looked after by my dear friend Patti. Tall and willowy, Patti had once been a June Taylor Dancer on *The Jackie Gleason Show*. I'd met her years before through her husband, Bert Murray, the Rutgers biology professor who, as you may recall, was a friend to Sam.

Patti loved Tiko, but the feeling was not always mutual. It was hard to know quite why, but I had my theories. For one thing, because Patti liked Tiko she tried to be friendly. From the bird's perspective, this came across as forward. Patti also wore her long blond hair piled up on her head, so Tiko didn't have the usual cue that "this is a girl," and she couldn't exploit his clear preference for women with long golden hair.

"If you'd only let your hair down you would have him eating out of the palm of your hand!" I said to her one day. But she never did adjust her hairstyle, so my theory went untested. She reported that while we were away he sometimes charged at her when she entered his room, although he tempered the assault—she was feeding him, after all. She gave up wearing sandals on Tiko visiting days, foiling his beak with sneakers and socks and wearing long pants to make sure her ankles were armored.

When we're away Tiko is confined to his room, although he's free to go in and out of his cage. (His room is fixed up so he cannot hurt himself—the rest of the house is not. It's a large room, with three big windows so he can watch the birds and passing cars.) When Patti looked after him, Tiko's room was immaculate. He's a social preener, and, unhappy with his substitute flock, he didn't preen when left alone with her. Soon after we came home there were feathers all over the house as Tiko began to preen anew.

When Mike returned from Captree, Tiko was particularly happy to have him back, although Mike felt an undercurrent of what he thought might have been suspicion on Tiko's part, as though Tiko imagined that Mike had abducted me and stashed me away in a faraway nest out of his reach. "What have you done with her?" Tiko seemed to be saying as he glared quizzically at Mike upon his return. His need for socializing, it seemed, was greater than his parrot's penchant for conspiracy theories, and he soon transcended his wariness.

He deigned to hang out with Mike, following him around the house and initiating their whistling duets. Attaching himself to Mike's big toe with one of his feet, he preened, running his beak through his feathers. Tiko wanted companionship, but if Mike reached down to give him an affectionate scratch, Tiko gave a small squawk and lunged. He strictly regulated the social contact with Mike. God forbid Mike should get the wrong idea and start to take liberties!

Tiko looks forward to Chinese takeout when I'm gone—Mike brings home Tiko's favorite dishes to ease the pangs of separation. As I've mentioned, I can't stand Chinese food. But both the men in my life have a real taste for it; without my steadying influence, they tend to gorge themselves. Tiko is especially gluttonous when it comes to peanuts, snow peas, and baby corn.

When I am gone they are two bachelors bravely facing the world together. But the parrot lacks his usual spunk and most nights packs it in after dinner, leaving Mike to fend for himself. Eight o'clock rolls around and Tiko decides he's had enough. He flies to his cage and expects Mike to bid him good night and shut him in. This is a far cry from his usual routine. Over the years, my bedtime has gotten later, and now his habit is to stay up with me until midnight, when the sandman strikes. "Bedtime, Tiko," I'll say. "I'm going to sleep." He obliges me and hops on my hand. I ferry him to the door of his cage and put him down. He climbs into his little abode and attains his perch. "Good night, sweetheart," I say. "I'll see you in the morning." His eyes never leave mine. He droops his head and half closes his lids. It's very quiet in the house. Very safe and secure for him. I close the cage door, for he sleeps better behind bars.

At Captree I'd call in most nights for the daily report. At first, Mike put me on the speaker phone, but Tiko became so agitated at the sound of my voice—running up and down his perch next to the phone, talking a blue streak—that we had to stop this practice.

His response to the speaker phone is par for the course. He's into instant gratification. To this day, when I come into the house and he hears my voice he screams until I come up to see him. If I call, "Tiko, I'll be up in a moment," he quiets down, but only for a minute. Then he thinks I've forgotten him and starts screaming again. The scream is the same blaring car alarm he emitted at Josie's, a deafening version of contact calls designed to travel a mile or more if needed, through dense jungle foliage. You can't miss it.

I PINED FOR TIKO while I was at Captree. But I didn't feel as far away from him as I did when I was in some foreign land. The park was on Long Island's South Shore, about a third of the way out, a two- to three-hour drive from home, depending on traffic. Its working environment was a far cry from the rugged blinds of graduate school or the minimal research stations of the tropics to which I'm accustomed. I sat at the edge of a parking lot under a beach umbrella, a hot dog stand at my back and a marina just across the way. Docked in the marina were a fleet of charter sportfishing boats that worked the estuaries or went out past the surf line for Striped Bass, Bluefish, tuna, and Mako Shark. The parking lot, which held hundreds of cars, would gradually fill each day. Over the course of the long afternoons the lot would slowly empty until I would be left almost alone, a few strag-glers beachcombing, surf casting, or coming in on a late charter.

I set up near the edge of the lot in the sand, infiltrating into the gull colony that was nestled in the dunes. I'd thoroughly scouted Cap-tree, marking the nests I wanted to watch. The nests were small de-pressions in the sand, about eighteen inches in diameter, lined with wispy Marram Grass, dried seaweed, stray bits of vegetation, and bright remnants of string and plastic from the garbage dumps nearby.

There were normally three eggs to a nest, light brown in color with dark brown and black splotches. The eggs stood out in the sand, but their coloration was originally a camouflage. The Herring Gull is a subarctic bird, nesting on rocky cliffs and tundra grasses. But it is the consummate generalist among gulls, and as human populations have increased along the coast of North America in the last hundred years, Herring Gulls have been drawn to the easy pickings of the hot dog stands, marinas, and garbage dumps of places like Captree, and have followed their human hosts south. Now their range extends from the Arctic all the way to North Carolina, and because they are larger and start breeding earlier than most other gulls and terns of the northeastern and middle Atlantic seaboard, Herring Gulls have been able to select the best nest sites for themselves and displace native populations.

The Herring Gulls at Captree ran to type. One pair had actually nested *underneath* one of the picnic tables by the hot dog stand. The nest was shaded and the gull couple and their offspring grew pudgy off a steady diet of junk food. The rolling dunes were littered with chicken bones from the fried chicken plates the concession stand served, and when the chicks hatched out, after twenty four days of incubation, it's likely that the first food they tasted was a hot dog with mustard.

I have painted a picture that perhaps gives you a somewhat skewed impression of my experience at Captree. It was not all fast food and asphalt. I quickly became subsumed in the natural rhythms of the gull colony. In fact, I entered a kind of trance two days before the chicks started to hatch out, and I began to hear them peeping in their shells. This was a signal for their parents to shift modes, from incubation (each taking a three- to four-hour shift on the eggs) to food gathering. The chicks' cheeps also enabled the parents to recognize their offsprings' calls soon after hatching. The chicks, too, benefited from hearing their parents while they were still in their shells, learning their calls sooner than if they had never heard them before hatching.

It took the chicks all day, using a little egg tooth attached to their top bill, to chip their way ever so slowly and laboriously out of their shells. (This small horn falls off in a couple of days.) I was in a state of high anticipation during this process. The whole colony seemed to be hatching out at once. Cheep, cheep, cheep, I heard. Chip, chip, chip, went their little beaks. The chicks emerged, sodden, bedraggled, pathetic-looking creatures. Madly cheeping, they stood immediately upright, their heads wobbling. Soon they were dry little brown-and-black-spotted bundles of fluff, their bill gaping open for food—utterly adorable.

I came back to my digs that evening elated. I was staying at the Scully National Audubon Sanctuary with Carl Safina, a MacArthur fellow and the author of the beautiful and much acclaimed book *Song for the Blue Ocean.* Carl got his Ph.D. under me at Rutgers and is a vice president of National Audubon. He managed the sanctuary and worked at the Scully Mansion, a huge, drafty old house with a spiral staircase, stone veranda, and expansive, elegant grounds, left to Audubon by the widow Scully.

Carl and I were good friends. When I returned to the mansion from the colony he often was preparing a dinner he had caught of fresh Bluefish or clams and mussels he had mucked in the tidal pools. We ate and talked about the vast ocean and the science of the creatures that lived in it. Captree was an idyllic time for me, up each morning before first light, a short drive across the bridge to the colony on the barrier island, and then all day with the birds.

Just in the way I had learned to appreciate Tiko's wild nature in the midst of our split-level house in suburban Somerset, so, too, did I realize that a bird colony that had survived, indeed thrived, on the edge of one of the largest urban areas in the world had just as much to teach us about nature and our relationship to it as parrots in the Costa Rican jungle. I loved the juxtaposition of the teeming, tumultuous lives of birds as humanity's incessant activity hummed all around. Also, because the gulls were used to people, they paid no mind to my chair and umbrella. I had the sea breeze at my back, and sunny blue skies overhead. Best of all, the marina had a bathroom. This was not Brazil, the outback, or Suriname, where I'd squatted among the scorpions and snakes.

I spent all day taking notes as I watched chicks toddle around near their nests, beg food from their parents, find shade, and avoid danger. As the days went by I forgot to eat. I found I never left my post, even to avail myself of the bathroom. I was riveted, absolutely enthralled. I didn't need to be hidden or confined. When the chicks hatched out I was simply part of their environment. The gulls ignored me, and I felt an immense sense of freedom. It was almost as if I had entered a deep state of meditation, so completely did my attention meld with their activity.

I apparently also ignored the ticks that were part of the gull environment. The ticks walked up one side of me and down the other, but so intent was I on watching the birds that I ignored them. Sometimes at night I'd take twenty-five or thirty off my body while in the shower. Then disaster struck. I found a circular rash just below my knee that looked like a sure sign of Lyme disease. I couldn't bear to abort the experiment; Mike and I had literally been working for years toward these results. We could have tried again the following breeding season, but I am monstrously impatient; it seemed like far too long to wait. I can be as stubborn as Tiko, and I decided to forge on, despite the Lyme. I'd had Lyme before, and the antibiotics did more to make me sensitive to sunshine than cure me. People are terrified of Lyme (it can permanently damage you), but I have the attitude that I'm always going to get better no matter what happens, so I didn't take it seriously. (This attitude infuriates Mike, by the way.)

Carl knew I was sick, but he didn't know how sick or he would have doubtless overcome the deference that nearly all students feel for their teachers and called Mike to come collect me. I also managed to hide my illness from my husband. He could tell I wasn't exactly feeling chipper, but I'd call him at night right before bed, when I would have been drowsy anyway. Little did he know why I sounded so exhausted.

Day by day my lethargy increased; I finally admitted to myself that I needed antibiotics, but if I'd told Mike that I was sick he would have made me return at once. May had turned into June, and July was fast approaching. I was exhausted, I ached all over, and the heat of the sun blasting against the white sand of the gull colony became unbearable. Still I hung on, until I was so tired I could no longer take notes or even sit upright.

After a particularly grueling day in the colony I knew I was shot, but I also knew I had stayed just long enough to get the necessary data. I drove home that night, having trouble staying awake at the wheel. It was a surreal journey, down the Belt Parkway, over the long expanse of the Verrazano-Narrows Bridge, the lights of Brooklyn and lower Manhattan glittering over the black water of the harbor, the Statue of Liberty with her torch ablaze, the car floating over the highway through the industrial wasteland of New Jersey's Meadowlands, just under jets taking off and thundering into Newark International Airport, back home to my husband and the parrot who owns me.

"Sweetie," I called out to Mike as I staggered through the door. "Where are you?"

He came running downstairs, his look of joy at my return quickly changing to concern as I collapsed in his arms.

Tiko gave a loud squawk, and the next thing I knew he was on my shoulder and so taken with my sudden appearance after so long an absence that he even forgot to peck at Mike, who was still holding me.

The boys put me to bed and Tiko assumed his position, up on the pillow, standing proud and tall. He didn't know anything was amiss. It was late and I was tired, that was all. But he may have picked up that something was wrong when Mike, not I, put him to bed. When I'm home that's my job.

The next morning, Tiko flew to the banister to resume our morning ritual. But when eight o'clock rolled around and I still wasn't up, he flew to the bed and preened my fingers and then my hair. When that didn't rouse me he became panicky, flying up to Mike, who was in the office, calling out to suggest something was wrong, then flying back to frantically preen me. I did get up that day to go to the doctor, and that temporarily ameliorated Tiko's anxieties. But when Mike and I returned I immediately flopped back into bed.

Mike cursed my pigheadedness, administered antibiotics, and made me as comfortable as possible. I couldn't stay awake for more than an hour at a time. I ached all over; walking to the bathroom exhausted me. I lay in bed, fading in and out of consciousness. Tiko spent his days standing quietly on the pillow by my head. He was beside himself with concern and couldn't fathom why I was bed-bound. He refused to leave my side even to go to the other room for food. Not even nuts and chocolates could entice him away. Mike brought us both our meals in the bedroom.

Tiko spent his days in somber vigil, leaning his head against mine and cooing softly. Mike returned one night from the office to find me sound asleep, my long, rather unruly mass of brown hair fanned out across the pillow. Tiko had spent the entire day gently separating and preening each strand, and laying each down on the pillow. He repeated this day after day, and I was often unaware of his ministrations because he was so gentle. Whenever I surfaced from feverish sleep, he was beside me, the pistachio green of his chest feathers and the emerald of his powerful wings glowing. He kept a watchful eye over me, his irises a flaming gold, his pupils black and unfathomable.

My nails grew shorter daily as Tiko incessantly filed them with his beak. His constant preening and undivided attention were his way of showing me that he wanted to take care of me. I'd been caring for him all these years, feeding him, sheltering him, carrying him around the house on my arm. Now I was immobile, helpless, completely vulnerable. Illness tests a relationship, and Tiko was there for me. His presence comforted me, and the depth of his devotion and his impeccable attention opened a great well of tenderness in me for him, just as I think my vulnerability opened a corresponding well in him.

For three weeks I was consumed with weakness and fever—three weeks during which Tiko refused to leave my side. As I became a bit stronger, he was willing to leave me for short periods, but only if I insisted.

"You've got to go upstairs with Mike to eat now, Tiko," I'd say. He would look at me balefully and half turn on the pillow, lifting up one foot and then the other. Mike would patiently wait.

"Go on, Tiko. Go upstairs with Mike."

Still he would hesitate, perhaps reaching down to gently preen my hair.

"It's okay, sweetie. I'll be here when you get back. Go with Mike."

He would grudgingly step on the stick Mike offered, craning to keep his eyes fastened to mine as Mike conveyed him from the room.

Finally, I felt strong enough to leave our bed and make my way tentatively to our kitchen table for a meal. Although I was quite weak, Tiko took this as the sign that I was finally on the mend. He was transformed. As I bent over the broth that Mike had prepared, Tiko swooped through the house, chattered and called, slid down the banister, flew back to his plate of fruit on the table, gleefully threw food on the floor, chattered volubly, initiated a whistling duet with Mike, and gobbled up pinyon nuts, which he had forsaken during my illness. Mike and I were stunned, so complete and sudden was his transformation.

By the dog days of August I had made a partial recovery. I was back to my old self, embarked on a plethora of projects, charging through my days. I expected Tiko and I to resume where we had left off before my illness. But his behavior toward me was forever changed. He wouldn't leave my side and became superattuned to my body language. His aggressive behavior toward me vanished completely. Our morning preening sessions extended from ten to thirty minutes. In fact, if I had allowed it, Tiko would have preened me for an hour or more each morning.

I think my sickness terrified him, triggering memories of Josie's mother and aunt. They'd become sick and gone away, and Tiko had been sent to live with Josie, which he must have viewed as punishment. Perhaps he was afraid the same thing was happening over again. He thought he was going to lose me.

In the wild, too, a long-lived bird that mates for life is devastated when it loses its other half. It doesn't go back about its business, but spends an inordinate amount of time looking and calling for its mate and haunting the nest they shared. The surviving bird sometimes isolates itself from its flock, and often neglects preening and caring for its feathers, putting its ability to fly efficiently in jeopardy. Such lost, forlorn birds can be seen just standing around, barely feeding themselves, letting down their guard, not doing the things they need to do to keep themselves healthy.

Although it is not documented in scientific literature, there is no doubt in my mind that the care, concern, and tremendous empathy Tiko offered me during my illness is commonplace in the parrot world. The only parrot native to the mainland United States, the Carolina Parakeet, was ruthlessly slaughtered into extinction nearly a century ago, in part because the highly social bonds of the animals made them particularly vulnerable to human predation, and the nurturing response that they share with other types of parrots to their injured flock-mates often cost them their lives.

Great flocks of Carolina Parakeets once roamed east of the Mississippi, lending a touch of tropical color to our landscape. Wheeling through the air in close formation, their long tails streaming behind them like colored ribbons, Carolina Parakeets were magnificent birds. Hundreds would alight together to feed, forming a carpet of rich green, orange, and yellow in our fields and forests. Can you imagine how breathtaking they must have been? Now they are gone forever.

Carolina Parakeets were so abundant that hunters blasted away without apparent effect, for sport, not food. The birds were sitting ducks. Glancing at Tiko, who is just a little bit larger but no more brilliantly colored than was a Carolina, I find it impossible to imagine killing such a beautiful creature. Unfortunately, sport was not the only reason the parakeets were killed. The birds had a taste for fruit and seeds; fruit growers regarded them as a plague and slaughtered them at every turn.

The parakeets' social predilections contributed to their demise. Whenever a gunner felled a bird or two, the flock would wheel around and hover over their fallen companion. Carnage followed. The birds were blasted out of the sky, and the more parakeets that lay dead or dying the more fervent was the flock's hovering. They wouldn't leave as long as one fallen bird was calling out in pain and fear.

The birds received federal protection, but it was too late. The flocks had become diminished and the remaining birds stopped breeding. This same pattern holds true for many social animals, including Redpolls (small Arctic birds), certain species of colonially nesting seals, penguins, Quelea, Ring Doves, and perhaps even Monk Parakeets. When the flock or herd falls below a certain critical mass of animals, the remainder stops breeding. There seems to be a hormonal feedback loop involved, whereby the calls of the males stimulate other males to call, which in turn stimulates hormone production in both males and females, which brings the females into breeding condition. Without the stimulation of many males calling, the females never reach breeding condition.

I would think this critical mass phenomenon would not hold true for human beings, even though we are intensely social creatures. The last remaining couple on earth, as did the first, would doubtless copulate. Would they be infertile? Perhaps the interbreeding that would necessarily follow would cause sterility or genetic problems. Our prohibitions against incest certainly have biological roots.

Since the demise of the Carolina Parakeet, ornithologists have discovered that playing tape-recordings of large flocks calling out to each other can sometimes induce birds to breed. We could have tried that on remnant flocks of parakeets, but we didn't have the science. In any case, there might have been something else in their plight at our hands that was driving them toward extinction. All the science in the world might not have been enough to save them.

The instinct to hover over a flock-mate who is screaming in pain may not seem evolutionarily sound. Wouldn't it make more sense to deduce "danger" or "trap" from screams of pain, and scatter? Among long-lived, highly social, pair-bonded animals with well-developed social systems, the urge to help, and the primacy of what can only be called selfless feeling or concern, prevails. Perhaps these imperatives are derived from our biologically wired sense of interconnection.

Elephants will return to an injured mate, as will primates, whales, and crows, to name a few. In the Gombe preserve on the northeastern shore of Tanzania's Lake Tanganyika, Jane Goodall has found that chimpanzee offspring will remain with their dying mother for several days—not leaving her side until she dies. Cynthia Moss found that elephants in Amboseli and other preserves in Kenya continue to visit and caress the bones of their departed relatives for several years. Other elephants walk by these same bones without notice.

I've even seen similar behavior in Franklin's Gulls. When one gull is shot down and injured, its flock flies overhead, screaming. It's hard to know why such behavior has evolved—it certainly did so before the presence of human beings with modern weapons. My speculations on selflessness aside, faced with a lesser threat than a man with a gun, sheer numbers could stave off an attack. A wild dog with a shrieking parrot pinned under its paw might well bolt if dozens of birds suddenly mobbed it (I think of watching the startled dog turning tail in Australia when the flock of Sulphur-crested Cockatoos took flight). A screaming animal is still alive, and so, conceivably, can be helped. The distress calls of an injured companion may also be related to the nurturing response of parents to offspring—when a young bird or primate gives a distress call, its parents immediately come to its aid, and can often save it from harm.

Parrot hunters, searching for birds to sell to the pet trade, exploit this instinct. They capture a bird, chop off its wings with a machete, and leave it in a tree to scream in fear and pain. When its flock comes to the aid of the injured bird, the hunters throw their nets. Needless to say, many birds are mutilated or killed during capture. Fortunately I've never seen these barbaric tactics—I think I might go berserk.

For me, both the pathos and the beauty of these stories is immense. What could a parrot possibly do to help a flock-mate who's been shot or had its wings chopped off? What did Tiko think he could do to help me? I was stunned by his capacity for empathy—stunned to see that his well-being was so wrapped up in mine that he refused to leave my side when he knew I was sick.

We tend to think of empathy, altruism, and the capacity to love as characteristics that are innate, an indelible part of our personalities. We say that so-and-so is a loving person or a cold person; we admire, are even awed by, people who have a large capacity for compassion. I think of Mother Teresa, Mahatma Gandhi, Martin Luther King, Jr. We think that our ability to love is the core of our humanity. We find out just how deep and powerful that core is in moments of crisis, pain, or joy. In these moments, the shell of our self can split open, and we find that our capacity for love suddenly seems limitless.

We are not alone in this. So it is with animals. Their capacity for intimacy and connection with one another and with us isn't fixed. It grows and develops. It has untapped depths and reserves. It can, perhaps, be taught. It is influenced by experiences and events. The relationships animals have with us are fluid and constantly forming and reforming. This was one of the most cherished lessons that Tiko taught me as I recovered from my illness. My fragility reconfigured and expanded him. It enlarged his capacity for love.

FINALLY, TOWARD THE END of the summer, I had the results of the lead analysis that I had worked so hard to obtain at Captree. They were fascinating. The behavioral defects we'd observed in the lab—in balance, locomotion, begging intensity, and avoiding heat stress—all occurred at Captree. Chicks with higher levels of lead stumbled more, and begged less often and less intensively than their lead-free siblings. But the chicks' disability at Captree was mitigated. It was true that a number of chicks had strayed and been cannibalized by their neighbors, and the lab report showed they did, indeed, suffer from high lead levels. This meshed with the results of our lab work, which indicated that lead exposure decreased chicks' ability to recognize their parents and nests. But it seemed that we also had a preponderance of very good parents at Captree, which closely supervised their chicks and successfully prevented most of them from wandering off to their doom.

We also found that other effects of high lead levels had been ameliorated, seemingly by conscientious parents. It took me months to fully recover from the Lyme, but before I did, and while I was still weak, we went back to the colony to catch and weigh chicks at fledging. We had to time it perfectly, both to get the chicks at the right age and because I was still sick. I had the energy for one more push and that was it. Mike, a couple of graduate students, and I ran down and caught all our banded chicks. We took feather samples and weighed the birds. As you can imagine, it was not an easy task. We looked like something out of the Keystone Kops, running crazily around hundreds of screeching gulls.

By dusk the deed was done, and that trip added another set of data to our work. We were surprised to find that in the field, unlike in the lab, the chicks all weighed about the same at fledging, regardless of their exposure to lead. It seemed that the parents were able to feed their chicks enough high-quality food to partially ameliorate its effects. Lab scientists usually assume that results in the wild will be more severe than those that show up in the lab; so the finding that parents could actually lessen the harmful effects of lead raised quite a few eyebrows.

We speculated on the reasons for the weight discrepancy between the laboratory and the field. Feeding sixty lab chicks is difficult. We gave them as much food as they wanted, but couldn't offer them much variety. Their diet was high-protein dog food and some fish. In the field, chicks are fed a wide range of foods, and it may be that the diversity of food helped them keep their body weight high. Then, too, perhaps gull parents are more persuasive than lab technicians when it comes to convincing chicks to finish their dinner. Typically a gull parent indiscriminately feeds its chicks, but in some cases I've seen parents splitting up their chicks, feeding the weaker ones off to the side. It turned out the parents didn't spurn their weak offspring; quite the reverse. In what we would think of as a very human gesture, they invested extra energy and attention to compensate for their chicks' disability, giving their weaker offspring that needed it a helping hand.

The results at Captree dovetailed neatly into the great lesson that Tiko had taught me during my illness. It's not always the survival of the fittest. The dog-eat-dog world is touched by gentler forces. The brilliant essayist and physician Lewis Thomas, in *Late Night Thoughts on Listening to Mahler's Ninth Symphony,* gives us his thoughts on why altruism should extend from us to the rest of the world.

"Altruism," he writes, "in its biological sense, is required of us. We have an enormous family to look after, or perhaps that assumes too much, making us sound like official gardeners and zookeepers for the planet, responsibilities for which we are probably not yet grown-up enough. We may need new technical terms for concern, respect, affection, substitutes for altruism. But at least we should acknowledge the family ties and, with them, the obligations."

Tiko has taught me, a sometimes headstrong and often ferociously independent woman, the importance of interdependence, the importance of taking care, and the importance of being cared for. It's a necessary part of being human and being connected to the world around us that we realize and acknowledge our vulnerability and the vulnerability of all creatures, and that we act in accord with that knowledge. It is critical that we allow the empathetic and altruistic part of ourselves to be the guiding force behind the way that we conduct our lives, whether we give to those less fortunate than ourselves, take care of the magnificent creatures that share our world, work tirelessly to preserve native habitat, or separate each strand of an unruly mass of hair so gently that we do not wake our loved one as she sleeps.

10

Birdbath

YOU MIGHT THINK THAT OUR RENDEZVOUS UNDER THE credenza, Tiko's gallant watchdog behavior, and, finally, his sticking by me during my illness denoted an unassailable intimacy, a closeness in which there was nothing left to be desired. Alas, as a biologist, I knew this wasn't so. The little imp was holding back, in his birdish way. There was a last bastion of trust we had yet to breach, and this was the bath.

You might also think I would have had enough of Long Island, watching birds in the blazing sun for twelve-hour shifts, and risking yet another bout of Lyme disease. Not so. I have an inexhaustible appetite for what may strike many as pure torture.

I was back on the Island's South Shore in the summer of 1994, hunkered down in a small canvas blind for five or six days at a time, watching a colony of one hundred pairs of the federally endangered

Roseate Terns at Cedar Beach. The Roseates nested together inside a colony of several thousand Common Terns, whom they closely resembled, except their bills were black, not red. Terns are small, about a quarter of a pound, with white breasts and gray backs. As colonial terns they are, in many ways, similar to the Herring Gulls. They lay a clutch of three eggs, which they incubate for twenty-two to twenty-four days (just short of the gulls), and are intensely social and territorial. But in their elegance and delicacy they are unlike the boisterous, chunky, opportunistic Norway Rats of the sky. The terns are specialized fish feeders, and they disdained the island's hot dog stands and garbage dumps. I perched in my blind, scrutinizing through binoculars the food parents brought home to their chicks. Mike and I thought the Roseates might be on the wane because something had happened to their food supply.

Cedar Beach was, as far as we knew at that time, one of the largest Common Tern colonies in the world. Now, however, not a tern remains. The Red Fox, which I tried in vain to get the town officials on the Island to live-trap and relocate, is to blame. Although the Red Fox was probably brought here during the colonial period so that displaced English aristocrats could blow their bugles and hunt with their hounds, locals on the Island insisted the foxes were part of the natural environment and pressured their elected officials into letting them stay.

I suppose there's poetic justice in the fact that the fox is now the hunter instead of the hunted. Terns traditionally nested on barrier islands because these islands were relatively free from predators— free, that is, until we connected them to the mainland with bridges.

The foxes crossed at night, and a colony of six thousand birds was reduced to zero in about five years.

The foxes didn't eat or destroy the nests of six thousand terns. A fox or two that only occasionally comes into the colony causes a minimal amount of damage by eating a few chicks or adults. But when foxes are regularly on the prowl, over an extended period of time, the birds desert their nests because of their ever-present sense of danger.

It was a pleasure to watch the terns while they were still around. They cruise twenty or thirty feet above the water, hunting for schools of killifish and other minnows. Their dives are stilettolike, deadly, unerring. They break the water with barely a splash and sail over the dunes on long, wispy wings.

I sat in the blind, looking out at the huge colony spread out over the lush grass into the open sand that stretched in front of sparse, stunted pines. It would occasionally cloud over in the afternoons. The terns would be lashed by the wind, wobbling and then somehow righting themselves in the unsteady air, blown backward as cool gusts flew up off the beach and the sound of thunder mixed with the sound of the surf. Then they'd row forward again into the gale, sliding out of sight against the lowering sky.

When a nor'easter came, the feeding terns came in off the water, returning to their mates, which had been brooding the chicks. The birds, all six thousand of them, fluffed their feathers and hunkered down into their nests, which offered scant protection—shallow, insubstantial indentations in the sand, even less developed than the nests of gulls. The terns brought their heads into their chests as the first fat drops drilled into the colony and popped off the canvas top of the blind, the chicks cuddling under their parents' wings, poking their heads out every now and again, the air salt-smelling and faintly fishy from the sea. Then the storm would start in earnest and all the birds would face into the wind, not their usual helter-skelter formation, all facing one way as if expecting something miraculous to suddenly appear. The wind buffeted them, and then the deluge ripped over and into them. The pounding rain drowned out the sound of the surf, and the dark gray sky and the ocean merged; everything was water and I couldn't see the nests that were right in front of my nose. I huddled in the blind. The wet canvas smell was very strong. The blind's walls rippled and snapped. Droplets condensed on the inside of the roof. I knew better then to touch them and break the seal. I closed my eyes. It was like being inside a drum. My thoughts left me and I found the quiet place inside myself, the safe place, the eye of the storm. I can't tell you how much time passed. Finally the barrage tapered, and the parent terns moved a short distance away from their nests and fluffed themselves in quick, exaggerated shudders. Moisture exploded off their plumage. And then they began to preen.

BACK HOME IN SOMERSET I thought about those storms and how the terns responded to their soaking. The terns' posture in the face of the kind of violent storm I've described was defensive, since if the birds had become soaked and the temperature dropped, they could have become chilled and perhaps died. The chicks were even more vulnerable because their down wasn't waterproof. But mostly the terns seemed to enjoy a shower, especially on warm summer days. So, too, apparently, did Tiko. We surmised that while we had been at Cedar Beach he had been surreptitiously bathing. We had placed pans of water in his room, which heated up during the day, hoping the urge to bathe would strike. We came home to half-empty pans and the newspaper we'd placed beneath them sopped. The bird had been busy with his ablutions. But the sneaky fowl refused to dabble so much as one toe in his pans when we were around to enjoy the show. Perhaps it was because there was plenty of preening going on when I was at home, which took care of at least part of the dander that collected in his feathers.

At last there seemed to be some chinks in his armor. I thought his furtive frolics in the water pans might indicate a willingness for more adventurous forays, but I refused to let my hopes get too high and then see them dashed. Whenever it thundered, he fluffed his feathers, just as wild parrots do to allow the rain to trickle down to their skin. Because this response to thunder seemed so clearly preparatory, we never lost hope, and whenever I showered I invited him to accompany me.

"Will you come with me, Tiko? I know you'd really love the shower," I'd say. I'd start the water running, then walk to the railing outside the bathroom where Tiko made his stand when he knew the shower game was afoot. Inevitably, his response would be the same: a special soft croon that I knew meant "No way, Jose," and a slight retraction of his head that expressed his effrontery at my ridiculous suggestion.

Guy had kept abreast on my progress with Tiko in this area, but he had softened in his regard for the bird after Tiko had one evening deigned to pick some butter off Guy's bread. Guy, of course, was delighted, and once the ice was broken they became fast friends. Now Guy plies him with all sorts of fatty foods, much to my displeasure.

"You know it's not good for him!" I scold.

"We all have to go sometime," Guy says, and grins. He really can be devilish.

Guy now shared my hope that one day Tiko would overcome his "phobia," as Guy liked to call it, and follow me into the shower.

Then, unexpectedly, everything changed. One hot summer day, in a hiatus with the terns, I turned on the water and went over to the railing. "Do you want to take a shower, sweetie?" I asked. To my amazement, Tiko stepped onto my finger just as if he had been doing it for years.

I reassured him. "Tiko darling, what a good, brave parrot you are. See, it's only water. Here, I'll make the temperature just right."

I thought as I got closer to the water he wouldn't go all the way, letting me bring him to the brink and then flying off as he had done once before. He watched my eyes, trying to gauge whether what was happening was really okay. "Tiko, I'm not going to hurt you," I said. "We'll both go in together." He didn't make a sound; he just held my gaze, quiet and a little bit scared.

I slipped out of my robe. I felt giddy, light-headed. As we neared the running water he began to raise his wings and fluff his feathers. I was sure he would bolt, but he held tight. I felt a tremendous warm rush. Together we stepped into the shower, and I slowly moved under the water, holding him away from the full stream. He was timid, clinging, nails digging painfully into my fingers—but he chose to stay.

I let just enough water bounce off the top of my head to splash onto his back. He spread his wings and rubbed his head on his back feathers as the water ran off him. Finally, he called softly; I knew he meant that he had had enough, and I carried him back to the bedroom to put him under a lamp. There he remained, warming and drying himself.

Our showers quickly became a shared ritual. Tiko wasn't always in the mood, and I knew better than to push it. But sometimes there was nothing he liked better. When I shampooed my hair I'd put him out on the towel rack. While the conditioner soaked in, back he'd come. He quickly learned that this second round meant we were almost done, and he was reluctant to leave, clinging to me with added tenacity. "Tiko, honey, we can't stay in here all day," I'd tell him. Afterward he'd stand under the lamp, an odd but workable substitute for the heat of the tropical sun, and preen himself as his feathers dried.

The showers were a far more significant barometer of his closeness to me than his courting and mating behavior. He was allowing himself to be placed in a position of complete vulnerability. If I dumped him under the full force of the shower, he would get completely soaked, and if it was cold in the house and there was no way to warm up, hypothermia might set in and he could die. Although there were no predators around, Tiko was still swayed by instinct. He wasn't bathing near the top of the forest canopy; he was four feet off the floor. With wet feathers his ability to fly was compromised. Should a predator enter the house, he would be completely at its mercy. There was a solemnity, a sense of gravity in my delight that he had finally let down his guard enough to enter the shower with me. As it always is with our most important relationships, when new frontiers of closeness and intimacy are crossed we feel inside ourselves the answering reverberations of new responsibilities that enlarge us, deepen us. So it was with Tiko. I knew that for him the shower had been a huge leap of trust. In his mind he was placing his life in my hands.

TIKO'S EXUBERANCE in the shower suggests that parrots in the wild approach their bathing with equal exhilaration, and that it is very important to them. I've watched this in Brazil on the Cristalino River, a small black water tributary of the upper Amazon, where many kinds of parrots abound.

I was on the Cristalino in 1999. The area had not been occupied by the early settlers to Brazil, or even by indigenous Indians. A few settlers moved into the river basin in 1976 to one of Brazil's planned towns, called Alta Floresta, which was set up to produce indigenous products such as cocoa, Brazil nuts, and guarana, a fruit drink. Small plots of the rain forest were cleared for agriculture and cattle. It was all very low-key until 1983, when gold was discovered near the Cristalino. The sleepy town swelled to 180,000 or more. Crime and prostitution were rampant. It took three years for the miners to strip the easy pickings of gold from the riverbeds and the forest floor; then they moved on. Today, the population of Alta Floresta is only about 28,000. Much of the rain forest in this river basin is now protected by the federal government. The ecotourism lodge where Mike and I stayed, as well as the surrounding land, is owned by the conservation-minded Victoria Da Riva Carvalho.

I had come for the parrots, of course, to be in the Amazon, and to do research on my long-term question of how parrots forage, on what, and their vigilance behavior during feeding. But I was also studying bird predation on butterflies. Smooth-billed Anis, all black and slightly larger than starlings, were capturing the butterflies as they came to the beach to sip minerals from the mud and sand. The butterflies gathered in dense groups, some as large as six hundred, and the anis skulked in to grab two or three before the group scattered. I was trying to determine whether a given butterfly had less of a chance of being eaten if it was in a large compared to a small group.

Our friends and neighbors Paula and Chris Williams were with us. Chris is a civil engineer technician, and Paula used to work in a medical lab. When the lab was downsized she took early retirement. She now has plenty of time to accompany me on walks in the woods that back up against our neighborhood, and to go farther afield. We share an interest in everything wild. I hadn't noticed that she had been watching me watching the butterflies.

"I can't believe you're going to sit here all day without moving," she said.

"So many things are happening. And all at once." I watched an ani grab a lovely swallowtail. "I have never found a place where it is so easy to watch creatures eating each other!"

"How nice for you!" She laughed and returned to the woods to search for birds.

———

IT HAD BEEN DRY in the jungle, but one afternoon the clouds were no longer white and billowy. The sky darkened and the butterflies I had been studying left the beach, flying erratically in small groups toward the safety of the deep forest. The winds roared, trees swayed; leaves, twigs, and old fruit pods littered the ground. I barely made it to the lodge before the torrent came. I swung in a hammock, chills going up the back of my neck as the forest looked like it was going to be ripped from its roots. At first I dismissed it as my imagination when over the roaring downpour I began to hear what sounded remarkably like parrots calling.

"Do you hear parrots?" I asked my husband.

"In this storm! Are you kidding?" He was swinging blissfully in the hammock next to mine, rocked by warm wet gusts that came rolling through the thatch-covered veranda of the lodge. "Why don't you come over into my hammock, and forget for a moment about your birds." But I was having none of it. The calls persisted. "I hear them. I'm going to investigate."

"You can't be serious."

I grabbed my umbrella. "Watch me!"

"Joanna," he pleaded. But I was already gone, off the veranda and into the storm.

The rain was warm, and it washed over my face. It was raining so hard that the ground was exploding beneath me; rivulets braided, frothed, ran away toward the river. I must have been a ridiculous sight, drenched to the bone in two seconds but still, ludicrously, holding an umbrella high above my head with one hand and grasping binoculars with the other, through which I eagerly gazed. That's why I was holding the umbrella, you see, not in an attempt to stay dry but because it offered a modicum of protection to the binoculars' *lenses,* without which I hadn't a hope in Hades of catching a glimpse of the raucous denizens of the forest; I followed with my ears, shifting directions, adjusting my course, homing in on them in the ocean of rain as their cries became louder and louder. I scanned the treetops, teetering with my umbrella like Mary Poppins, and then, suddenly, there they were. I had found the ultimate birdbath.

In the winding branches of the Ype trees above me, I counted two Scarlet Macaws, thirteen Chestnut-fronted Macaws, and two Blue-headed Parrots. The Scarlets were glistening, almost prehistoric in their size, close to three feet tall. The smaller, delicate Blue-headed Parrots were Tiko's stature; indeed they are closely related to him. Instead of Tiko's red, their foreheads were a delicate deep blue, but otherwise they were a rich and varied green—the basic parrot palette.

These were the noisiest Psittaciformes I had ever heard, and that's saying a lot. Their calls seemed pitched to excite; they worked themselves into a frenzy, shrieking with glee. Spread wings and open bills drank in the falling rain. Their eyes were closed and they were hollering. They looked like tiny, brightly colored umbrellas with their wings flaring. They twisted their heads every which way, craning their necks, and then I started laughing as they flipped over to hang upside down, flapping their wings madly so that their undersurfaces were exposed, beating their wings furiously as if to propel the moisture through their feathers, deep into their flesh. Even in their excitement, the pairs remained close together, watching over each other, stopping occasionally to scan for predators.

This was the first real rain they'd had in three months, and it was an ideal time for it to be raining since it was the middle of the day. The storm was brief, lasting only about twenty minutes. They flew to another Ype tree by the dock to preen in the emerging sun. The tree was ablaze with brilliant yellow flowers, brighter than buttercups. The parrots were drenched, but they still could fly, although perhaps not far. They preened in pairs, only inches apart, running their beaks through the feathers of their wings, backs, and tails. They preened themselves for a few minutes, then allopreened, gently pulling the feathers of their mates through their sharp bills. They mostly worked on each other on the same body area: neck, back, or tail. They even preened under the tail, intent on oiling their feathers, preparing them, protecting them. Brown Capuchin Monkeys rummaged around in the trees and shrubs below, but the parrots ignored what I could easily distinguish as the monkeys' sharp "look out for the predator" calls. The monkeys may have been responding to a snake in the lower branches of the nearby trees, or an Ocelot on the forest floor. I couldn't see anything—the jungle was too thick. Looking up, I did see a small falcon, but it was not big enough to worry the monkeys or the birds.

One pair of Chestnut-fronted Macaws preened each other for nearly an hour. Suddenly they stopped, made eye contact, and then the male, with his head bent low, climbed onto the female's back. The female averted her tail, and he slid his tail under hers so that cloacal contact was made. If they were vocalizing, it was so quiet I could not hear it. He dismounted, they preened, and then he mounted her again. It was almost as if the romance of the rain, the intensity of the sensual experience of bathing, had precipitated sex. After the second go-round, they moved about a meter apart, preening themselves, and then, with chattering, squawking calls, lifted off, flying over the treetops at a great speed, perhaps searching for a suitable nest site.

As if stimulated by the macaws, the Blue-headed Parrots also began to court, preening and billing each other around the head. Within minutes they, too, were copulating. Their contact was brief. I felt sure the rain had signaled the beginning of the intense courtship phase of these birds, triggering ancient physiological changes inside them—increases in the sex hormone that lead to enlarging testes and ripening ova. The rains pointed them toward mating, finding a nest, laying eggs. For my entire career I had wanted to watch wild parrots in this intense courtship phase. To find two species simultaneously mating was breathtaking.

THE BRAZIL TRIP was one of the dozens I'd taken since Tiko's arrival in Somerset, and he has had to get used to bossing around a number of surrogate flock-mates when I travel, which is rarely easy for either him or the lucky person charged with his care.

When Mike and I were off to Kenya to study the behavior of Cattle Egrets that forage with zebras, buffaloes, and wildebeests, I entrusted Tiko to Bill Boarmann, a graduate student of mine who lived nearby and had raised an assortment of birds. After we'd gone, Bill came to feed Tiko with his wife, Jeanie, and their daughter, Kaitlin. Tiko has a "thing" for small children, and he likes blondes with long hair, so Bill was obviously the intruder in the bunch. Without so much as a warning Tiko flew at Bill, who shielded his face with his arm. Bill ran from the room, assuming his wife and daughter would follow. But Tiko had approached Kaitlin and climbed onto her lap, where he preened and softly cooed. He'd move away when she reached out to touch him, but would quickly climb back up. Had an adult male tried to make a similar move, Tiko would have chomped him mercilessly. Tiko was apparently mesmerized by the young child's beautiful hair. He watched her eyes and softly called, a soliloquy of love, no doubt. It was nearly a half hour before Kaitlin's mom pried her away. Bill was still smarting from the small nip Tiko had given him, and he was miffed that his wife and daughter were enamored of Tiko, so enamored that they all returned together for the next feeding, which resulted in a replay of the same scene. Tiko clearly wanted Jeanie and Kaitlin to feed him, preferring that Bill stay home. And indeed, as often happens, Tiko got his wish—for the rest of the month only Jeanie and Kaitlin came to play with him. Eventually, Tiko preened Kaitlin's fingers and hair, though he never let her preen him.

In the first few years after Tiko came to live with us, we tried a number of strategies for Tiko's care when we went away. When we went to Florida to visit Anne and Alex, we sent him to Josie, with dreadful results. We had naïvely thought that perhaps Tiko would forgive and forget. No such luck. He greeted the poodles with a tirade, rushing to the side of his cage and badgering them by calling, "Hello! Hello! Hello!" nonstop. They soon fled from the room. Then Tiko screamed nonstop for five days. There goes the neighborhood. He must have thought we were giving him back to Josie—horrors!

He adjusted immediately to being back home after this experience. He strutted through the house, calling provocatively to reestablish our contact. He showed me each of "our" nest sites, even though it wasn't the breeding season. He often does this when I return from a trip. It is his way of reasserting our bond after a separation. But he only needs to do it once, and then he settles into our normal routine.

On our next trip, we knew we couldn't leave him with Josie, and we were reluctant to leave him cooped up in a cage for so long, even though he seemed to prefer this to being sent away. We arranged for a friend to come in periodically, feed him, and sit with him a spell; so we set up a room for him where he could be free to fly from perch to perch while we were gone. The only available room where he couldn't wreck anything, get stuck behind bookshelves, or injure himself on sharp objects was my bike-riding room. He knew it well, so we thought there wouldn't be a problem. We diligently parrot-proofed it, removing all objects that could fall on him and pulling furniture from the wall so he wouldn't get stuck behind it. We spread out newspapers to protect the rug and built several new perches for him, one of which we wedged between the two corner windows so he could gaze outside and watch the birds.

Several days before our departure when all was ready, I put out his favorite foods and brought him in to see his new deluxe accommodations. He was so obviously anxious when he saw his cage in a new place and all the changes in the room that I stayed with him for a while, proofreading a manuscript to give the illusion of normalcy. He climbed into his cage and sulked with his feathers fluffed. I stayed with him for several hours, but he refused to eat or to leave his cage. As darkness fell, he hunched down in the cage's corner, still refusing to eat. I said good night softly and left him. In the morning, he didn't come to the railing and wake me in our usual routine. Instead, he stuck to his cage, with the door wide open, silently staring ahead. For three days I tried to pamper him into coming out or eating, to snap out of it, but he just sulked. When I presented the stick he dutifully climbed on, and I transported him to his new perch by the window. But he simply transferred his class-A sulk to this new perch, then flew to his cage, climbed down its side and through its door, and resumed his vigil on his old familiar perch.

After day four we admitted defeat and carried the cage to his old room upstairs. Immediately he began to drink and to eat a few sun-flower seeds—and within minutes he had flown to his perch by the window. For the first time in four days he solicited preening from me. He clearly wanted his old room back; he did not want to be banished somewhere else. He reacted as if we were punishing him; instead, he punished us by being sullen.

Over the years we have provided more and more protection for him when we leave. We installed an electric heater in the wall of his room. Now, if the oil furnace goes off while we are away, the electric heater kicks in, ensuring that he will remain relatively warm. He can stand some cold, but not prolonged freezing. My brother John told us about a device that reports the temperature in the greenhouses. We eagerly bought one and hooked it up to our telephone. All we have to do is call home from anywhere in the world and it tells us the time and temperature, and whether the electricity is working. People have complained because they call and get a report on the weather inside our house. I suppose that could be annoying. But we can always ascertain whether Tiko is warm.

THE FINAL CHAPTER of the shower saga, and the moment where Tiko's and my bond was finally complete, took place only recently. It came about, as these things tend to, in a roundabout way. Mike and I went off on another of our trips, this time to Indonesia as part of our research into worldwide patterns of how lead, mercury, and cadmium were distributed in bird populations, and how this affected behavior. Just as we had done in Australia with cockatoos, we planned to collect Cattle Egret feathers for later analysis (on other trips, we had taken feather samples in Australia, New Zealand, Hong Kong, China, Hawaii, and Costa Rica).

This project was a natural outgrowth of our Captree work. Now we wanted to understand how contaminant patterns varied worldwide, and discover if they'd reached high enough levels to affect behavior. This type of "biomonitoring" is fundamental to assessing when and where to take corrective action.

As I packed for the trip, I explained to Tiko that Patti was going to come feed him and check up on him.

"You must be nice to her, Tiko. She's your friend."

In response, he waddled over to my suitcase lying open on the bed, climbed in, and plopped himself down in the middle of my clothes.

"Sweetheart, you can't come. You have to stay here."

He answered with a soft croon and his most beguiling eyes.

"Come on, sweetheart, you have to get out of my suitcase so I can finish packing."

With a few more soft croons he slowly climbed up the edge of the suitcase and perched on its lid, turning to face me. I put a piece of paper beneath him to catch his droppings, for I knew this would take a long time and he would not leave me to pack alone.

"That's better, Tiko. You can stay there while I pack."

He crooned softly, fluffed his feathers, and settled in.

OFF WE WENT to Bali, Sulawesi, and Halmahera. Bali was the most populated and developed of the three islands. The landscape has been almost entirely sculpted and shaped by people into terraced rice fields on which no machinery was used; so the metals showing up in egret feathers should have been put there by atmospheric deposition, except, of course, for lead, which can come from the gasoline used by cars and trucks.

We traveled with a group of birders, mostly from the United States. The trip was organized by Ben King, who regularly leads birding trips to Asia. The logistics of the trip were daunting: lodging had to be procured in places where there was no tourist infrastructure; island hopping, by small plane or boat, had to be orchestrated; drivers had to be hired, food brought to field stations. Mike and I were relieved to have someone else handling the difficulties of travel; we could concentrate on our work.

We were in good hands with Ben. He is the author of the definitive *Field Guide to the Birds of Southeast Asia*. I'd known him since I was a graduate student at Cornell, where he was doing his Ph.D. under Charles Sibley, one of the foremost taxonomists in the world. Sibley left Cornell for Yale, and Ben went with him. But Ben was always more interested in fieldwork (learning about his subject firsthand) than in writing up research, so he never finished his dissertation.

Ben is slightly older than I am, tall and thin, with dark hair and brown eyes. He is always immaculately groomed and his clothes starched and well-pressed in the field. Over the years he's helped support himself by teaching ballroom dancing. He's a health nut, and carries vitamins and large plastic bags filled with fruits and nuts into the field. Birders treat him with awe. Ben can hear a snatch of birdsong and identify the bird before the rest of us have heard it singing. Hands down, he knows more about the ecology and natural history of the birds of Asia than any other person alive.

The uninformed tend to think bird-watchers are doddering hobbyists; but the hard core who take trips led by experts like Ben hike on steep, rocky terrain, are drenched by storms, stay in primitive lodgings, and often discover tremendous amounts about a species' distribution, range, and population size. Scientists can't get everywhere—not enough time, too many birds. Amateurs they may be, but intrepid birders are adding to our knowledge. They're doing science.

SULAWESI, UNLIKE BALI, still has some land covered with virgin forest, but it was, and is, disappearing at a rapid rate. Early one morning our small group trekked quietly into the highlands, searching for some of the island's treasures: Purple-bearded Bee-eaters, Snowy-browed Flycatchers, Yellow-billed Malkohas, Rusty-breasted Cuckoos. Mike and I, of course, were also intent in finding Cattle Egret feathers.

I fell behind the group, as I often do, because I like to take photographs for my courses at Rutgers. I was stalking a particularly lovely and elusive butterfly, a Blumer's or Black Swallowtail with brilliant, iridescent blue-green bands on its wings. I inched forward, finger poised to depress the shutter, when suddenly I found myself sliding downhill on the slippery mud. One of my boots somehow became caught; my foot stayed still, my ankle twisted inward, and I heard a crack, like a chopstick snapping in half. I fell to the ground and pain shot up my leg, sometimes in such intense bursts that I almost threw up, sometimes causing me to nearly pass out. As long as I sat still, I told myself, it was bearable.

I had fallen near a mountain stream. The water tumbled down the ravine, the sound of it soothing, mixing into and diluting the drilling pain. The landscape was wet, lush, gentle, in stark contrast to the fire inside me. Birds called in a cool wet world, the butterflies continued flitting through the foliage, water cascaded down the mountainside, a gentle wind stirred the forest. All continued as it had a moment before, but suddenly my world was vastly different. Or was it? What had changed?

Mike came back before the others to find me. "Darling," he said, kneeling down beside me and with great gentleness taking off my boot, every little move of the injured foot making me think I was going to pass out or throw up, until finally the boot was off. He took off his shirt and wrapped it tightly around my ankle, using a binocular strap to keep it taut, and then set my leg on his day pack so it was elevated. He calmly asked me questions, in his soothing doctor's manner. We both knew that in all likelihood it was a break, and after a quick examination Mike also determined that I had torn muscles up and down the leg, although he spared me this information at that point.

For those of you who aren't birders this may sound strange, but I then insisted that Mike go on with the others so he didn't miss anything of the wonderful birds we had come to see. The pain was so intense I wanted to be alone, and to at least feel that Mike was going to see some rare species for both of us.

"I can't go on without you. I'll stay here," Mike said.

"We've traveled halfway around the world. I'd kick myself if you missed what we've come so far to see!"

This little speech was delivered through clenched teeth. Mike had to smile at the image of me kicking myself with my one remaining good foot.

"I can't leave you."

"Please, sweetie. Catch up with them. One of us should see the birds. I'll watch the butterflies and birds here. Leave my small notebook."

He eventually left, and I tried to distract myself by drawing ferns and flowers; but my heart wasn't in it.

———

WHEN THE OTHERS RETURNED, Mike carefully unwrapped his shirt from my ankle. The leg had swelled and the flesh around the ankle and up the shin was black and blue and puffy as a boxing glove. I buckled over with pain and nausea as I tried to stand. When my injured leg brushed lightly against some foliage I nearly fainted.

"Grab her," Ben said. "She's going to fall."

Mike and Ben supported me on either side, half carrying me down the jungle trail. I hopped along, unable to put any weight on my injured leg. We stopped every hundred feet. I was exhausted, the pain was increasing, and they were having trouble holding me because of the steep incline and mud. We finally made it to the Jeep, and it took some minutes to load me in, because I couldn't move: the whole leg had swelled and was excruciatingly tender.

It was twenty-five miles back to the old logging camp that served as our research station—twenty-five miles of rutted mountain roads. I managed to note how beautiful the landscape was, the lush dark green of the jungle falling away down the hillside; gaps in the foliage revealed long views, down to the lighter green of the lowland, terraced fields. This journey, which would have been a pleasure under other circumstances, turned into a nightmare. The Jeep's top speed was ten miles per hour; even so I was tossed and jolted, blinded with pain. Tears streamed down my face, and I lowered my head so no one could see me, especially Mike.

"Joanna, are you all right?" For the first time, I heard anxiety in his voice. But I was in too much pain to answer. He wadded up his sweatshirt and rain jacket to stabilize my foot.

"Should we stop?" he asked.

"No, let's just get there," I said through my tears.

He stopped asking, but he made the driver slow down so the bumps weren't so bad. Another stream, another log bridge, more potholes and puddles. Darkness fell and the frogs begin to ratchet up.

IT WAS PITCH-BLACK when we finally arrived at our humble abode—wooden platforms for beds, the bathroom a hole in the ground. The Jeep could only get within one hundred feet of our cabin. Between me and rest was rough grass and a deep ditch. While Mike and Ben discussed how best to get me there I dropped to my knees, held up my injured leg, and crawled through the wet grass. When they turned around I had already gone twenty feet. They trailed along behind me, trying to help. At the ditch I used my good leg as a wedge and sat on one side, and then the other, swinging my bad leg up. It took me twenty more minutes to get to the cabin. I lay down on the hard board bed. All strength left me, and I was immediately asleep.

The bathroom was a problem—with just one functional leg, I couldn't crouch down, and the walls were so far apart that I couldn't brace myself with my arms. Mike scrounged up a pail, and together we were able to point me in the right general direction. There was an element of humor to this, but it was overshadowed by the grinding pain. Aside from using my bucket, I lay as still as possible while we tried to figure out how to get me into Palu, the nearest town. Fortunately for me, Mike had broken his left ankle the previous year in Brazil, and he had decided that we would never again be caught in the field without an air cast (I know what you're thinking, but when you consider how many times we've been in the field, our record of breaks, sprains, and illnesses doesn't actually look that bad). The plastic device had two sections, which fit on each side of my ankle. The leg was so swollen that the Velcro flaps barely met. Mike fed me some pills that dulled the pain to a dense throbbing.

In the time-honored tradition of fieldwork, one of our two Jeeps had just broken, so we couldn't take the only working vehicle and leave everyone else in the bush. Somebody might have fallen ill—you can't leave five or six people with no means of escape. I was injured but not dying. It took two days to fix the Jeep, and by the time Mike and I had arrived at the Mission Hospital in Palu I think we had both become quite expert in the use of the pail. "You know, these kinds of experiences are the glue of a marriage," I said, during one particularly trying maneuver. He just looked at me askance.

The hospital, a one-story concrete structure at the edge of town, was clean, but there was no doctor in the house. His rounds of small-town hospitals would bring him back to the Mission in two days. The nurses wheeled me around on a gurney. Our Jeep driver, Harry, translated their Javanese into English. They had an X-ray machine but no technician. Mike persuaded the nurses to let him use it.

The ankle was broken, no surprise. Back into the air cast it went.

"I'll need crutches," I said through Harry.

The Mission had no crutches; there were none on Sulawesi, as a matter of fact. We custom-ordered a pair from a local cabinet maker. I drew a crutch and labeled it with my measurements. Sixteen dollars American took care of the X ray. There was no charge at all for the attending of the nurses and orderlies since the doctor was absent. Exhausted, we took leave of the Mission's kind staff. Now all that was left to do was find a hotel and await the crutches.

We pulled up in front of the Golden, Palu's only hotel. Wouldn't you know it, all the rooms were on the second floor, and there was no elevator. I made my way around the hotel room using a wooden chair for a walker. It pleased me to have a toilet to sit on and a bed that wasn't a board.

Two days later and forty-five minutes before we were due to depart for a distant part of the island, the crutches were ready. The cost? About sixteen dollars, the standard charge, it seemed, for service in Palu. The crutches had a rustic elegance about them, and they were just the right height. But I couldn't get my fingers through the grips. We hadn't thought to measure the width of my hands.

Mike and I began to laugh, and then we were doubled over. The whole adventure was a farce. What next? Mike filed out the holds, and I hobbled to our bus, and the crutches became a treasured momento in a Somerset closet.

I realized, rather belatedly, that I was in no condition to chase down Cattle Egrets, and it would take some time to get a flight home. I began to think about what else I might study. While the group scouted for exciting, unusual birds, Harry and I toured Sulawesi's small coastal fishing villages, looking for chickens. We'd drive around until we saw chickens foraging in somebody's yard. Using a stop-watch and a pad, I recorded how many times a minute they stopped feeding to scan for predators. Vigilance, my friends!

I continued working with chickens. Curious bystanders approached the Jeep wherever we went, peppering Harry first with questions, then advice. There were many local bush doctors to be recommended, especially one who lived in the village of Tador, on Halmahera. He was renowned throughout Indonesia for his bone-fixing prowess.

"How does he cure you?"

Harry put the question to an old woman bent over in her yard. A barrage of Javanese came back, accompanied by elegant movements of her hands, which were lined with a thousand seams, their color as though they had been steeped in tea.

"He rubs your leg with oils from the forest throughout the day," Harry translated, "and if the pain is too great, he rubs the table with oil instead."

We went to Halmahera by ferry, but I never did take the cure.

OUR SULAWESI BASE CAMP had been grim, but it was nothing compared to our camp on Halmahera. The land was uncleared. It was gloomy and dark even at noon. Our bathroom was a hundred muddy feet of twisting trail behind the bunkhouse through a dense jungle. Mike came to the rescue and bought me a nice new shiny red pail of my very own. And to think, some women get perfume and jewelry as gifts from their husbands! They don't know what they're missing.

Ben had also made a distressing discovery. He and the group had found clear-cut hillsides near camp. The Indonesian government was enticing people to leave overcrowded Java and relocate on Halmahera. It had leased its land to Japanese-owned logging companies who were building roads to get at the timber, clearing land that would be used for farming, opening up the interior in their wake.

I was not the only member of our group who could not bear to watch television programs that open with animals in beautiful settings and close with chain saws and bulldozers—and here it was happening outside our back door. I was particularly concerned about Halmahera's rich parrot population. Although poachers are a serious problem for wild parrots, a far greater threat to their well-being is habitat destruction. All over the world the large tracts of primary forest that most species of parrots require are disappearing, felled by loggers, ranchers, and slash-and-burn farmers. The big-bodied parrots (cockatoos and macaws) need large holes in large trees for nest sites. These trees are disappearing at an even more rapid rate than the forests themselves, because they are the first that loggers cut.

In poor areas of the world, people are vulnerable to outside money—from the pet trade, from logging companies, from export agriculture. Unless wealth is somehow redistributed, these problems will persist and worsen. Ecotourism is the key. When a country's population realizes that it can get more money from tourists willing to pay to see a rhino, or birders who want to see a Scarlet Macaw, they will conserve their natural treasures.

The clear-cuts soured all of us, and my ankle was obviously not getting any better, strapped, as it was, into the air cast. It was still quite swollen, painful, and black and blue. I heard bones crunch whenever it happened to move—when my crutch caught in the mud, for example, and I lurched forward, putting weight down on the injured foot, which made me shriek with pain. We decided to abandon Halmahera, but with one thing and another, it was two weeks before we touched down on the tarmac in Newark. As you can imagine, I was happy to be home.

THE ORTHOPEDIST put me in a cast for six weeks. Tiko found this problematic. He'd been delighted to see me, and he didn't want to let me out of his sight, in case I was planning to disappear again or that wretch of a husband was plotting another one of his abductions. Tiko climbed on my hand and waited to be ferried around the house, his usual privilege. He'd look up at me and call softly, but when I'd extend my hand downward to grasp the crutch, off he'd slide. I tried him on my shoulder, but each time I lurched forward, he'd topple forward onto my chest, hanging frantically upside down by his feet. He'd scramble back up to my shoulder, I'd take another step, and kerplunk, off he'd go again. He became increasingly agitated, loudly calling, scrabbling against me, trying to find purchase. He wasn't getting his usual valet service, the physical contact to which he was accustomed, and he didn't know why.

When he did figure out I was injured, not spurning him in some way or slacking off in my responsibilities as his mate, he became solicitous. He walked behind me, keeping out of the way of the crutches. If I told him where I was going, he flew there first and

awaited my arrival. Our early morning preening ritual became dou-
bly important to him. He watched me very closely as he sat on the
banister in the dim light of early dawn. He was intent on letting me
sleep as long as possible, and jealously guarded the door. In the past he
had occasionally become overly enthusiastic, mistaking my tossing for
wakefulness, and had disturbed my slumber. Now he recognized that
I was injured and needed to rest.

When he was sure I was awake, he gently preened my fingers,
and I rubbed his nape. Our usual ritual called for about ten minutes
of allopreening. Then he would start to get hungry, and his beak on
my fingers would become almost like a nip, indicating that he was
ready to go eat. When I was in my cast, his gentle preening persisted
for however long I stayed in bed. And for the first time, I realized how
important these intimate morning moments were for me; it was our
time together, not just his, as I had believed for so many years.

I couldn't get my cast wet, which meant no showers. This proved
to be a problem for Tiko, who had grown to adore a good shower. He
wouldn't go in with Mike, so he became dustier and dustier and
spread dander through the house. I doubted whether he would go
into the shower without me, but I thought I might as well try. Mike
wrapped my leg in a plastic bag to keep the cast dry, and came into the
bathroom with us, in case we needed him.

"Come on, Tiko, time for a shower," I softly coaxed. He climbed
on my hand. I adjusted the water temperature, and held him at arm's
length near the spray. I expected him to fly away, but he clung tightly,
anxiously watching my eyes.

"It's all right. I want you to go in without me."

He looked at me and softly crooned; I was barely able to hear him.

"Please, Tiko, I want you to have a shower."

He continued to look at me, crooning a bit louder, the end of each croon rising in inflection, as if in a question.

"Yes, sweetheart, stay where you are and I will put you in gently."

Miraculously, he began to fluff his feathers and raise his wings. I slowly moved him into the shower's gentle stream. It had been nearly two months since he'd last bathed; he was so excited that he almost fell off my hand. The water ran off his back in tiny silvery beads. He flung his wings out and rubbed his wet head against his back. He was acting in the same manner as the bathing parrots I'd seen in the Amazon. We had finally made it. Tiko trusted me enough to go in by himself. He was just a little ball of green feathers, but at that moment I loved him so fiercely I thought I might scream, let loose my own call of exuberance and ecstasy through the Somerset jungle. The water rained down on him and misted my hair and cheeks. There was nothing that was withheld. Our bond was complete. Mike and I looked at each other without speaking. I held Tiko up into the water and he clung tightly to my hand.

Epilogue

BEING OWNED BY A PARROT IS, AS I'M FINDING OUT, A commitment beyond anything I could have imagined when Tiko first came to live with me. He was a boyish thirty-year-old bird when he arrived in Somerset, unhinged by the recent loss of his beloved Libby and Freda, cast into a strange environment, his world and his life turned upside down. His appearance is ageless. He looks no different now than when he first joined our household. But now he is almost a dominant fifty, a stately and majestic creature, sure of his position in the world, with clear ideas about how I should behave.

I am not allowed long absences. Three weeks is an acceptable period for me to "fly to the other side of the jungle," but then it's time for me to come home. This is not always convenient for a field biologist. Fortunately, we've found a caretaker whom Tiko adores. She is Paula of the long golden-red hair, a characteristic in a woman that always seems to make him weak in the knees. When she arrives, he rushes toward her, gently preens her shoes with his beak, seductively croons, and gazes love-struck into her eyes. His friendliness toward her fades, however, after my three-week limit. He charges toward her in a halfhearted attack. Softly calling his name soothes him, but soon even that fails.

Tiko will probably be around through our retirement. We might have liked to travel in four- or five-month stints, but he would be heartbroken if we stayed away that long. He is not a child one raises, who then becomes independent. He's part of our family; we have to consider his feelings, what's best for him.

Tiko's amorous behavior toward me has intensified through the years, and the hot summer of 1999, which mirrored the weather of the Costa Rican jungle, seemed to set off biological changes in him that kicked our courtship dance into overdrive. He frantically tried to find just the right nest site and discovered the small space beneath the bedroom dresser. It was a dark secure place, too small for predators such as the ubiquitous Somerset wild cat to enter. Since it's in the bedroom, it provides him an opportunity to make home improvements and keep a watchful eye on Mike while he woos me with a steady stream of coos and plaintive calls.

Its position gives him a strategic advantage. Early on in the summer he tolerated Mike, as long as Mike did not sit too close to me on the bed and kept his feet off the floor. If Mike went to the bathroom or put a tape in the VCR, Tiko scooted from his vantage point under the dresser and wildly attacked Mike's toes. His courtship intensified as the humid days stretched to weeks, until he was barely interested in food. When I worked upstairs, he needed preening every few minutes. He flew back and forth between the bedroom and the office, trying to draw me down toward the boudoir with long, raucous calls, followed by low crooning that I could barely hear.

Parrots don't go through menopause, and most female birds keep producing eggs as long as they live. But perhaps there is a human correlative here. As we get older, our sexual passion may wane, but often we become emotionally closer to our mates, less distracted without the pressures of career, child rearing, the financial responsibilities of a mortgage and college tuition. Our dependence on the person with whom we share our life deepens; we come to know each other's thoughts. We share an intuitive connection that goes beyond mere familiarity. Our lives are joined.

I feel that same sense of connection developing with Tiko. In the past couple of years I've often been called to National Academy committee meetings in Washington, D.C. I usually take a six-thirty A.M. shuttle from Newark. I dislike waking up so early, but it means I get to spend the night at home. Unlike Mike, who wakes up in time to get me some breakfast and kiss me good-bye, Tiko hates rising before daylight. When I pop into his room to say good-bye, he merely coos a soft answer, and goes back to sleep.

With the first light, however, he realizes I have gone, and gamely goes upstairs with Mike to eat a little breakfast of apples and Cheerios. Not too much, just enough to get by. He perches by Mike's computer, and follows him around the house. Mike is part of his flock, after all. He makes do. While Mike is out, Tiko sleeps. When Mike returns, they converse, complaining of my absence. Tiko follows Mike downstairs, eats spaghetti. They whistle a bit, as if to assure themselves that the world is okay. Tiko preens, but finally flies to his cage, deciding to wait it out. Perhaps I'll come home that evening.

But the meetings spill over; it seems there is always more to be done. Day two of my absence, Tiko breakfasts and then waits for me on the hall railing. When I fail to appear by noon, he flies to his cage and eats a few of the sunflower seeds he normally spurns. Mike assures him that I'll soon be home, but Tiko sits, silent, hunched over, refusing to make eye contact. Evening comes, his room grows dark, and he sleeps.

Meanwhile, I am making my way back to Somerset. The plane roars through the night. The taxi from the airport drifts along the dark highways. The meetings have exhausted me. I'm spinning from all the discussion, the problems we face, the endless travel that seems to be my lot these days. I drag myself through our front door. And there is Tiko, standing on the railing at the bottom of the stairs. Calling softly, he flies to my shoulder.

"I don't know how he knew," Mike says, "but ten minutes before you walked through the door he opened his cage in the dark and flew to the banister, calling softly for you. I looked, but there was no taxi outside."

Tiko's eyes never leave mine. "Don't worry, sweetheart, I'm home," I say. The spinning stops. I'm back with my family, my loved ones. I carry Tiko upstairs. How did he know when I was going to arrive? I have spent most of my life devoted to science. But in recent years my relationship to Tiko has begun to give me glimmers into another realm. There is so much we have yet to grasp about our connection to each other, and Tiko and I are joined in ways I don't begin to understand.

THERE IS NO SUCH THING AS OWNING A PARROT. You can't have a parrot as a pet. A dog, certainly, a cat maybe, but a parrot, never. Quite the contrary; you are the pet, and parrots vary in their ability to make good masters. Be warned—being owned by a parrot is not for the faint of heart.

NOTES:
1. Tiko is a Red-lored Amazon of the Costa Rican race, which does not have the yellow facial markings found on some of the other races or subspecies of Red-lored Amazon.
2. Chocolate is normally not good for parrots, as it can overstimulate the heart and is rich in fat, but in his early days Tiko was insistent. He has largely been weaned from chocolate, and now prefers sweet corn as a treat.

IN THE SILENCE OF THE NIGHT, I WAS HUNCHED OVER MY computer, answering letters written to Tiko and pondering questions about parrots. I am fascinated by the musings of my readers, and I diligently answer each one. I enjoy hearing the tales of other besotted parrot companions, and I arrange the letters neatly by date in a giant notebook. Someday, when I have time, I will fashion another tale around them, a kind of love-in for parrot companions.

Loud mooing sounds came from another room. I ignored them, thinking Tiko was merely trying to call me to his favorite nest site, under his cage in his bedroom. As long as I could hear him, he was obviously safe. As with small children playing in another room, soft sounds usually indicate all is well; it is silence that is disquieting.

Some of the letters I receive are addressed to Tiko. One reader even sent him special muffins made with his favorite fruits, which he ate while making loud comments on my inability to provide such treats. Adorable photos arrived via e-mail, attached to wonderful letters. Most inquired about Tiko's health, and how Mike and I are faring. "Is he still courting you as much?" "Has he seemed to age at all?" "Do Paula and Patti still care for him?" "How can I be as patient so that my beloved parrot feels safe and secure?" "Will mine ever preen me as gently or tenderly?"

One person even wrote proudly of an Amazon parrot who was fifty-seven years old and was also a rescued bird. Many people asked whether Tiko was paper-trained, a subject I did not address in the book. Some people put it bluntly: "How do you deal with the mess?" Others merely commented that they "keep our parrot in a cage most of the time to avoid the mess and feathers scattered about." I never considered confining Tiko so; he loves to fly around the house, whether seeking me out or returning to his cage to sulk if I do not behave properly. Early on we worked out a mutually agreeable arrangement: I praised him mightily whenever he "let go" while sitting above papers put there for that purpose, and he responded by flying to such perches when he felt the need. For years he has flown to one of five wooden perches I keep around the house for him—his special "privacy places," where I regularly change the newspapers.

In a rush of wings, Tiko flew up to land on the back of my chair, still crooning softly, drawing me away from the task of answering letters. Ignoring him, I continued writing. He preened my hair impatiently, and then abruptly flew back downstairs, squawking for me to follow. The calls continued, louder and more insistent, until I finally went to investigate. I found him peeking out of the door of a little red castle sitting on our bedroom floor. His eyes peered into mine, he gave his most beguiling croon, and he swooned lower, nearly touching the floor with his beak.

While cleaning out a storage room at Mike's parents' house recently, we had come across this wooden castle his uncle Pete had made for him when he was a child. The red paint had faded, but the small castle doors still swung open easily and the tower rising from the center was handsome. Struck with nostalgia, we carried it back home and placed it on the floor in our bedroom. It was a familiar piece of Mike's childhood, and in those grim days following the attacks of September 11, 2001, we were all seeking the comfort of a safer time. Even Tiko seemed upset by the images of burning buildings collapsing. For days, he sat behind my head on the pillow, alternately preening my hair and staring at the television screen. When I emerged from my mourning to work in the garden, Tiko watched me from the window, quieter and more somber than usual. We were both uneasy with the acrid smell of smoke and ash that drifted across the Hudson to our Somerset, New Jersey, home.

At Tiko's insistent chanting, I lay on the floor near the castle and extended my hand. "What is the matter, sweetheart? Are you still upset?" He walked to my side and delicately preened my hair, pulling each strand through his bill. He lay his head against my cheek and remained still, crooning so softly I could barely hear him. We remained so for a few moments, while I thought about the comfort such a small creature could provide, and marveled at his understanding of my pain. Slowly I moved my fingers, the glint of turquoise and silver rings catching Tiko's eye.

He delicately placed his foot on my finger and began to dance around and around, his body lowered, his head dipping up and down, courting me. This was unusual since his breeding season normally stops in late August. His need for added attention was no doubt due to his anxiety, and to my own. He gave long, loud, piercing calls whenever I was out of sight, frantically flying from room to room until he could land on my shoulder or sit on my ankle. Primates and parrots share a high regard for the importance of grooming and touching. We respond to trauma by wanting more contact. Touching transmits deep feelings we may be unable to express in any other way—a primal need to be one with others.

Slowly Tiko danced around my finger, dipping his head to choke softly. Then, staring into my eyes, he ducked into the door of the castle and disappeared in the darkness. I heard the soft crunch that indicated he was modifying the interior.

"No, Tiko, you can't do that. Mike's uncle built it over fifty years ago—you can't tear it apart. I like it the way it is."

He came back out to peer into my eyes as if to inquire just who I thought was building our nest, him or me. And then he quickly disappeared within, returning to his task. Surely I could appreciate the importance of making the inside of the nest just right. He began to work in earnest, tossing small bits of wood in all directions, and I realized I had to find a way to stop him before he destroyed more. I left the room, calling to him, and he quickly followed. After an hour's time of working at the computer, with Tiko sitting quietly behind me, I slipped downstairs and shut the castle door.

"Time for me to go to the office, Tiko," I called, and he quickly flew to the top of his cage, watching me get dressed. When I put on my shoes, he climbed down the side of the cage and entered, pulling the door closed behind him. He feels safer with the door closed, and he always naps when I am away. After all, if he had to stay up until well after midnight while I worked on my computer, he'd best grab a quick nap.

As I unlocked the door to my office at Rutgers, I heard Sue's anxious call, and then her soft grumbling as I put my books on the desk. Sue is a Nanday Conure that I just adopted. A student found her on the top of a building, abandoned and starving; her color was poor, her weight low, her bill broken, and her morale destroyed. With time, good food, and love, she has recovered her brilliant green and blue plumage, and her head is now a vibrant black. Even two different types of casts have failed to fix her bill, but she easily eats bananas and other soft fruit. She has even learned to dip Cheerios in her water bowl to soften them up before eating them. She lives in my office because Tiko would not tolerate her at home; my Somerset home is Tiko's, and no other bird better darken the door.

I brought Sue home just once, before taking her on the *Today* show. (I couldn't risk taking Tiko; with his unclipped wings, he might have flown into the upper reaches of the studio, never to be captured.) Tiko was not pleased. Somehow I thought I could sneak Sue into the downstairs bathroom, where I had once locked Hester the chicken, but I was dreaming. As I carefully carried her cage into the room, she gave one loud, piercing call, summoning Tiko from several rooms away. I quickly locked the door, but not before Tiko landed angrily on my shoulder and began roughly pulling my hair.

Tiko squawked loudly, and Sue answered, which set up another round of complaints on both sides. I shut the light off on Sue, which shut her up, but Tiko continued to complain fortissimo. He sat on the washing machine, staring balefully at the door, daring me to enter. Since Sue was safe, I simply went upstairs; true to form, Tiko followed. When Tiko was in bed, I crept downstairs to tell Sue good night, giving her time to grumble softly to me.

In the morning, Tiko immediately flew downstairs to check out the bathroom, and when he was unable to enter, he screeched loud enough to be heard a mile away. Only by sweet-talking him could I coax him upstairs for his breakfast, and only then by giving him his favorite, strawberries and cream. Usually I don't feed him such rich treats, but his feathers were definitely ruffled.

I locked him in the upstairs office, and got dressed just in time for the limo. Sue was delighted with the ride into Manhattan, watching all the passing cars and tall buildings and mumbling softly in my ear each time the car lurched forward. In the waiting room, she enraptured everyone with her excitement over the trays of melon and strawberries, bagels and cream cheese, and little chocolate cakes. She tried them all while waiting for her appearance.

She was a delight on the *Today* show, walking up and down my arm, calling softly when spoken to, and preening my hair gently while I was interviewed. She even fluffed her feathers and bowed to my interviewer, Ann Curry. On our return, however, I had to quickly remove her to my office. She is quite happy there, for she has me for five or six hours each day, and has entirely taken over the office. Bob and Carline, my technicians, are smitten by her, and she adores them.

With time, she decided that my office belonged only to her and I remained there at her pleasure. When I was alone, she happily walked about the top of her cage, exploring the bookshelves and amusing herself by pushing the books to the floor. She rode around campus on my shoulder, grumbling softly in my ear. Students were often taken aback by her loud squawk when they came too close to me, and they didn't make that mistake a second time.

Each week Sue took over more and more of my office, defending it against any intruders. Like Tiko, she adores women, and scowls whenever any male enters her domain. She is usually silent for a few seconds, but then begins to shriek loudly until the offending male leaves. One of the letters to Tiko asked how parrots identify a girl from a boy. Both Sue and Tiko seem to do so using visual and vocal cues. They immediately respond to long hair and a soft voice. Sue adores Bob, my graphics engineer, who has lovely long hair, and makes an exception for his male voice. And, like Tiko, Sue adores Mike. She is far too young to think she needs to defend me against Mike, and is content to allow him liberties Tiko will not tolerate.

Now, instead of being ruled only at home by a curmudgeony forty-seven-year-old parrot named Tiko, I am also governed by a demanding adolescent Nanday Conure who lives in my office. I find her cheery countenance comforting, look forward to seeing her, and sneak into the office each weekend to spend a few moments with her. The only trouble is, I feel as if I am having a workplace affair. Tiko, however, seems untroubled by this intrigue, as if it is a fleeting dalliance of no particular import. Perhaps parrots in the wild also have special friends they visit from time to time. This thought is enough to send me dreaming about working in the wilds of Peru, in search of Tiko's roots.

ACKNOWLEDGMENTS

MANY FRIENDS HAVE ENCOURAGED ME TO WRITE ABOUT Tiko and have provided helpful comments along the way. I thank them now: Michael Gochfeld, Michelle LeMarchant, Guy Tudor, Bernadine Chmielowicz, Ronald Barfield, Gail Buckler, Carl Safina, Jorge Saliva, M. Weinberger, and the many students and technicians Tiko has beguiled. Guy Tudor has been sending me articles on parrots ever since he met Tiko and decided he was spoiled rotten, and I have used many of these in my musings. However, Guy will never forgive me for leaving out certain details that have enlivened our conversations over the years. Tiko and I both thank Patti Murray and Paula Williams for their affection and willingness to visit and care for him in my absence. They put up with his occasional aggressive behavior in defense of his territory, and they serve as part of his extended flock.

I'd like especially to thank Kenneth Wapner of Peekamoose Productions for working creatively and enjoyably as my personal editor, for making the connections, and for helping me bring Tiko's story to a general readership. I want to thank my niece, Jennifer Wolfson, who helped me sort through and refine a once cumbersome manuscript— I will always treasure working with her. I also thank Ivan Gold for editorial assistance, Gail Ross (my agent) for her support, invaluable contacts, and expertise, and Bruce Tracy for shepherding the manuscript through Villard; without all of their help, Tiko would still be sitting on the shelf, his story unshared.

I was profoundly influenced by Donald Griffin's early book *The Question of Animal Awareness* (Rockefeller University Press, 1976); he provided a framework for recognizing the awareness and emotions of animals. Irene Pepperberg was also an inspiration; her research on the learning and communication of parrots has demonstrated their cognitive abilities. More than twenty-five years of teaching animal behavior has taught me the importance of drawing parallels between the behavior of humans and that of other animals—an approach I take in this book. Though "science" sometimes frowns on this approach, it is often more wrong than right to deny our common behavioral heritage.

My parents, Melvin and Janette Burger, were always supportive of my love for wildlife, and my brothers (Melvin Jr., John, and Roy) and sisters (Tina and Barbara) and nieces and nephews were a source of inspiration. My parents-in-law, Anne and Alex Gochfeld, encouraged me to write for a wider audience. Finally, our children, Debbie and David, accepted Tiko into our household with amusement—they, too, are part of his extended flock.

I owe my love affair with Tiko to my neighbor Jose Steinbock, whose fundamental love of animals and enduring patience kept Tiko safe. She immediately knew that Tiko and I belonged together, and gave him to me so many years ago when her mother and aunt died, leaving him alone. She is referred to as Josie in the book because some early manuscript readers were confused, thinking the name referred to a Hispanic male.

Most of all, I thank Tiko and his predecessors for providing many hours of love, companionship, amusement, and insight, and my beloved husband, Mike, for being there for all of us. He puts up with Tiko's occasional ill humor, my long hours of working endlessly at the computer, and my need to sit in bird blinds for fifteen hours a day watching the behavior of parrots and other wild animals. Without Mike's love and attention, this book would have been written much sooner, or not at all.